Break Rank,
Make Bank

www.thecashflowcommando.com

Break Rank, Make Bank

A Bullet Proof Guide on Using
Your Military Benefits
to Make Real Money

Michael Balboa

Break Rank, Make Bank
A Bullet Proof Guide on Using Your Military Benefits
to Make Real Money

Copyright © 2021 Michael Balboa

ISBN 978-1-956904-04-8

Printed in the United States of America

Published by Blacksmith LLC
Fayetteville, North Carolina

www.BlacksmithPublishing.com

Direct inquiries and/or orders to the above web address.

Dedication

This book is dedicated to my parents, sister, and brother-in-law—my solid rock foundation. Without you all, the floods surely would've swept me away. Additionally, I'd like to thank everyone I've learned from along this journey. I'm a firm believer that wisdom is attained through counsel, and this book evidences the value of the counsel I've received from so many.

"Break Rank, Make Bank"

For duty and honor I serve with glee,
a call to action and a life of thrills.
Ready for what my nation requires of me,
but why the struggle to pay the bills?
Spurning retreat, still I ponder,
"What is it that I must I learn?"
Life has placed me in a puzzle.
I want to serve, but I need to earn.
The conventional path simply won't do,
I see its bearing; I must Break Rank.
I've committed to purpose, I'm on my way.
I'll tell you one thing, I will Make Bank.

Contents

Foreword

Time is the great equalizer, rich or poor, we all have the *same* 24 hours in a day.

Do you seek to achieve *financial independence...* to eventually become *independently wealthy*?

Break the mold of relying solely on "climbing the organizational ladder" to increase wealth (*Break Rank*). Create income stream(s) additional to your military service income, while enjoying the unique aspects of military service (*Make Bank*).

As an Active Duty, Reserve/Guard, or Veteran service member - have you ever assessed your service-connected income, benefits, and/or entitlements? If not, you *should*. The very process of evaluating your military service benefits/advantages will help you understand your service-connected strengths – in addition to your occupational credentials and capabilities. The *Break Rank, Make Bank* real-estate investment framework aims to help *you* succeed at leveraging your service-connected benefits for long-term financial success.

The author, Mike Balboa, is a current US Army Special Forces service member, who currently practices and explains his paradigm-shift journey in this inspiring, humble, and humorous book - *Break Rank, Make Bank*. Mike offers a modern, proven, "turn-key" education on how current/former US Military service members can effectively leverage the "no/low money down" loans such as the Veteran's Affairs (VA) home loan, Navy Federal Credit Union, and similar loan products, via an accurate, digestible, and actionable framework to achieve financial independence. The *Break Rank, Make Bank* framework enables investors to accumulate wealth faster, requiring substantially *less* startup investment capital, with repeatable success.

Mike and I met in the Special Operations Forces (SOF) community. Over time, we realized our complimentary and often synergistic perspectives on personal excellence, many of which are subjects in my forthcoming book. Financial independence and personal excellence "domains" are inextricably linked. Given Mike's assessment of my experience, he felt compelled that I present a few perspectives on personal excellence with *you*.

Prior to meeting Mike, I served in the Active Duty US Air Force (USAF), from 1999 to 2009, separating as a Technical Sergeant. My final military assignment was as an Enlisted/Officer Accessions Recruiter in the Detroit/Greater Detroit, Michigan area. As a recruiter, I improved my understanding of human needs and wants, while witnessing the transformational power of military service. After service, I remained in the US Defense sector as a DoD Information Technology contractor, from 2009 to the present (2021). I've directly supported the US Air Force, Army, Navy, Marine Corps, and currently, US Special Operations Command components.

My combined 21-year military and contractor journey exposed me to CONUS/OCONUS, South West Asia, South East Asia, European, Pacific, and African locations - enabling wartime and other-than-war objectives. During this journey, I've integrated, and applied the lessons of many personal development courses, methodologies, books, conversations, and other media sources, in pursuit of defining a lifestyle system of personal excellence. This experience imprinted the habit of observation, open mindedness, win-win dialogue, compartmentalization, and selective, best-practice habit integration. As a result, I've interacted, inspired, and successfully influenced hundreds of US service members, civilians, contractors, and expatriates over the years. The contents of this foreword represent some of the relevant and empowering advice I've presented to my dynamic audience.

The freedom of replacing our financial requirements with income from real-estate (passive income), expands our ability to define how we'll earn *active* income. Passive income enables us to start a business or perform a job for the *actual enjoyment* of the work, over the need for its salary. When our passive income can sustain the financial requirements of our lifestyle, we gain *far* more free-time and willpower to do *what* we want, *when* we want; leading *our* lives on *our* terms.

If you're an Active Duty, Guard/Reserve US service member, financial independence permits you to enjoy your career/profession without the absolute *need* to "make rank" in order to "make bank". You can enjoy your role/rank, while your financial capacity grows with great decisions made, year over year. I've personally witnessed several people develop financial independence in pursuit of long-term wealth, which in turn, permits them to create their chosen life, while further developing their wealth. Many of these wise people either started, ended, or continue to develop and enjoy their military/professional careers, as financially independent Americans. *Break Rank, Make Bank* reveals how *you* can join the "ranks" of the financially independent, *while* serving in the US Military.

The *Break Rank, Make Bank* and financial independence paradigm shift includes the realization that your life's purpose does not have to be, *solely funded* and/or *defined* by your primary profession (day job/active income). The benefits of multiple income streams can enable you to work on an unrealized life interest - requiring additional resources to cultivate. Should you choose, multiple income streams can advance your primary profession, by offering the means to invest in continuing education and/or the ability to pursue/expand entrepreneurial opportunities. While not a "get-rich quick" scheme, multiple forms of income (earned, passive, portfolio) enables money (and time) to work for you, instead of you working *solely* for it.

The American Dream (Way of Life) morphs with *each* generation.

Today's American Dream: the *freedom* and *capability* to define, lead, and live one's life without persecution.

Such freedom is genuinely expressed when one achieves financial independence, with aspirations to achieve independent wealth. In my international travels, the many people I've encountered desire the freedom to lead their lives, provide for their families, in peace, with *accessible* prosperity.

Preserving the American Way of Life starts with *you, your* paradigm, and *your* choices. Realizing the American Way of Life, requires Americans (all people) to embody effective principles, values, and stewardship; ultimately leading to continuous refinement of high-performance habits.

"First you make your habits, when your habits make you." – Conan Valente

Mike and I seek to help you understand that true, long-term financial and personal development success requires a long-game, whole-person approach when defining the habits necessary to achieve your desired end-state. "Doctrinally sound" choices when repeated, form high-performance habits, *defining* one's character. High character people adopt judicious principles and values, yield relevant visions and goals, then subsequently *produce* repeatable and sustainable achievement. Recall the prominent habits military service introduced, reinforced, and *rewarded*. Great military/society influencers were primarily governed by their own, high-quality, high-performance habits, forging high-quality character, as the *underlying* fabric of their lives.

"You can't *depend* on your plans for *tomorrow*, until you *consistently* choose to master your behavior, *today*." – Conan Valente

However, habits are not fixed and often, require ongoing, conscious attention. Once habits are formed, habits continually reinforce our *previously* established priorities and perspective. To realize a fulfilling life, we're challenged to continually improve, evolve, and validate our chosen life direction and underlying habits. Therefore, we must continuously manage our habits to effectively *serve* our present *and* future.

One's own limiting beliefs play a *significant* role in undermining financial and personal excellence actualization. I've witnessed many think *only* in terms of one's immediate limits. In the context of military service, I remind compatriots on the following world-view check:

"Don't let your 'rank' get in the way of your 'success.'"
– Conan Valente

I've observed many limit their success, creativity, and forward-thinking potential - by stating "I'm only a <insert rank/role here>", therefore limiting even one's imagination to proceed with solving a problem or pursuing a dream. While I'm not advising service members act inappropriately, rather, when possible, don't view your respective situation from the lens of your *current* limits. Often, thinking *outside* your limits, eventually leads to a way-forward from your current foxhole (position). Words and thoughts matter; appreciate and cultivate your unlimited potential by thinking accurately, decisively, and creatively. The world needs you to lead by example, manage up, and out!

During my mentoring sessions - I've often said:

"Where you *start* does not *have* to be where you *finish*, in life." – Conan Valente

This is another point where you don't let your "rank" (present situation) limit your success. In the case of Mike Balboa - he didn't let his *initial* "junior-enlisted" roles, narrow or limit his success. Instead, he leveraged his strengths, while systematically strengthening his weaknesses. Mike pursued a *relevant* education in finance, built a well performing real-estate portfolio, and continues to realize his potential through steadfast habit and momentum management. Mike completed his undergraduate degree, became an elite USSOF Operator, amassed over $100K in annual real-estate passive income, and became a published author - while in his 20s! From the inception of his grand-vision, Mike made quick work of his foundational personal development, in *five short years – he was ALL IN!* This intense, focused manifestation of achievements was made possible because of the effective embodiment of habit, character, and self-worth; mobilized to pursue relevant and rewarding aspirations.

Fortune favors the bold. Living the experiential/experimental mindset is a *bold* virtue.

Mike Balboa embodies a high-road, experiential, and experimental mindset in all aspects of his life. Regarding real-estate, Mike's goal-commitments were reaffirmed when he validated his deductive, problem-solving approaches in real-estate investment and management. As an example, Mike accounts that *each* investment property market assessment, property procurement, and tenant management process, was an opportunity to refine his management approach, while creating a knowledge/experience artifact to support the next "experiment opportunity". This was evident even upon experiencing *temporary defeat* - in the case of a house flip that didn't profit anywhere close to what was planned. Mike learned from his many *experiments*, reflected on his *experiences*, *refined* his plans, and *committed* to apply the lessons learned/knowledge gained to the *next* investment *experiment*.

This approach reminds us to *not* strive for perfection, rather, evolution. By doing so, we persist through challenges as we let our *inevitable* shortfalls, mistakes, and delays, "roll off our back" - teaching us lessons. The outcome of Mike's experiential/experimental approach has formed *Break Rank, Make Bank*; a fusion of vocabulary, concepts, processes, and *experiences* applied as validated *experiments*, forged into a proven, comprehensive real-estate management acumen. This *validated* framework enables you to *accelerate* the creation, quality, and potency of your real estate empire-building experiments, experiences, and outcomes.

"Every master, was once a disaster."
– T. Harv Eker, Secrets of the Millionaire Mind:
Mastering the Inner Game of Wealth

Foreword

In the pursuit of evolving my own human maturity, I've been validating various human performance systems, of which I'll briefly share the following concepts: *"The Four Pillars of Self-Worth Development"* (abridged) and *"The Lesson of Pole, Pole"*. Mike and I hope the following content will help advance your personal excellence *and* financial independence journey.

The Four Pillars of Self-Worth Development:

In 2015, during a period of physical isolation and deep introspection, I created the basis of a personal transformation framework titled: "The Four Pillars of Self-Worth Development". To obtain a visual read-ahead of *The Four Pillars*, please refer to *Figure 1* to obtain understanding.

Since then, *The Four Pillars* concept has been validated and well-received by a broad audience. *The Four Pillars* guides practitioners to assess our current life-situation, with the intent of taking decisive action in pursuit of life fulfillment. *The Four Pillars*, summarized:

1) *Leverage* Strengths
2) *Strengthen* Weakness
3) *Eliminate* Distraction
4) *Eradicate* Self-Doubt

The Four Pillars of Self-Worth Development

> **P1 | LEVERAGE *STRENGTHS***
> Outward Facing, Defines Us, Generates Wins
> *OPPOSITE* OF SELF-DOUBT | "I CAN"

Self-Doubt Continuum

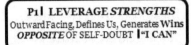

> **P2 | STRENGTHEN *WEAKNESS***
> Avoidance, Anxiety, Workarounds, Excuses,
> WEAKNESS REMAINS | "I STRUGGLE"

> **P3 | ELIMINATE *DISTRACTION***
> SELF-DOUBT CREATES MORE DISTRACTION,
> DRAINS CAPACITY, WEAKNESS HARDENS TO
> SELF-DOUBT WITH EACH OCCURENCE.

> **P3 | ELIMINATE *DISTRACTION***
> UNWARRANTED DISTRACTION,
> PROCRASTINATION DELAYS PROGRESS, MASKS
> PROBLEM(S), BUSY **NOT** PRODUCTIVE.

> **P4 | ERADICATE *SELF-DOUBT***
> Inward Facing, Defines Us, Generates Loss
> *OPPOSITE* OF STRENGTH | "I CAN'T"

Decompose Self-doubt To Permit Weakness Conversion To Strength... Path to Life Fulfillment, Freedom

Unchecked Weakness becomes Self-Doubt Path to Unfulfillment, Regret

The Four Pillars of Self-Worth Development

- Pillar #1: *Leverage* Strengths
  - o *Identifying Factors:*
    - ▪ What actions/tasks do you say: "I can do...", "I'm good at...", "I like to do..."?

- Typically, strengths represent our interests, capabilities, most intuitive work - your best foot forward.
- First response to challenges, basis of favorable reputation.

○ *Personal Development Actions:*

- Assess your strengths. Employ as often and accurately as possible.
- Leverage strengths as temporary offset/workaround to weaknesses.
- Pair strengths with weaknesses to generate lessons-learned from strength-employment; aids weakness strengthening.
- Document findings and experiences.

The Self-Doubt Continuum: An insidious cycle of unresolved weakness, left unchecked, becomes a *lifestyle* of long-term failure and personal compromise. Pillars 2, 3, 4 from a subordinate cycle, limiting the realization of our potential. Pillar 3, "Eliminate Distraction"- includes behaviors of *unwarranted* (unintended/unproductive/untimely) distractions and procrastination; regarded as action and task *avoidance* behavior. We then tend to procrastinate, distract ourselves, or allow ourselves to be distracted. Eventually, when we don't attempt to strengthen the weakness, unresolved weakness *becomes* self-doubt, over time, forming a "virtual-limit" to our capabilities.

- Pillar #2: *Strengthen* Weaknesses
  - *Identifying Factors:*
    - What actions/tasks do you say: "I struggle with ..."?
    - Signified by conditions where the weakness/self-doubt *adversely* impacts your life, prevents progress, and/or requires a workaround.
    - When the weakness is encountered, one feels internal resistance/doubt, anxiety develops, avoidance measures (distraction) are chosen *over* addressing the weakness.
  - *Personal Development Actions:*
    - Identify *what* causes internal conflict, low interest, temporary defeat.
    - Assess your limiting beliefs.
    - What unwarranted distractions are chosen in favor of weakness? Why?
    - Consider performing the weakness under your best conditions; "break the ice" developing weakness-to-strength *conversion* momentum.
    - Pursue projects that include weakness *and* strength activities.

- Alternate strength and weakness tasks (task interleaving) execution to help leverage momentum in weakness conversion.
- Do the work, the process may need to be repeated, document findings.

- Pillar #3: *Eliminate* Distraction:
  - *Identifying Factors:*
    - What actions/tasks do you say: "I'd rather do this..."?
    - Weakness spurs *unwarranted* distraction. Unwarranted distraction is often an activity or skill which we feel confident in performing, even if inappropriate. Non-progression excuses result, weakness remains.
    - Upon weakness encounter, we self-distract to the point of busyness and/or temporary pleasure. Failure excuses result, weakness remains.
    - The distraction/procrastination behavior ultimately increases stress and anxiety, further reduces work capacity and desire, limiting maturation.
  - *Personal Development Actions:*
    - Track/journal distraction events, potential root causes, and triggers.

- Experiment/research ways to interleave constructive/warranted distractions with weakness and strengths.
- Ward off lower priority/impulsive tasks; consider block-time planning.
- Identify temptations leading to (bad) habits, research damaging impact to progress. Commit to change and self-reward when temptation is *denied*.
- Improve whole-person health. *Some* distractions could be indicators of health imbalance. Consider "Pomodoro Method" work/rest cycle.
- Do the work, the process may need to be repeated, document findings.

- Pillar #4: *Eradicate* Self Doubt:
  - *Identifying Factors:*
    - What actions/tasks do you say: "I can't do ...", "I'll never be good at..."?
    - Unresolved weakness "crystallizes" as the *antithesis* of strength.
    - One changes *life direction* leading to perpetual self-doubt task avoidance.
  - *Personal Development Actions:*
    - *Start* by defining weakness/self-doubt areas which *greatly* limit your life.

- Research/state the importance of self-doubt to strength conversion in relation to your vision/goals.
- Apply lessons from *effective* resources, with frequent experimentation.
- If necessary, limit other activities to focus additional resources to dismantling/eradicating your highest-priority self-doubt.
- Surround yourself with influences aligned with desired outcomes.
- Do the work, the process may need to be repeated, document findings.

Converting one's weakness and self-doubt to strength, means tackling the challenge - *step by step*, continuously improving.

The Lesson of "Pole, Pole":

In June 2021, I hiked/bicycled up and down Mount Kilimanjaro (Tanzania, Africa), under a constrained and very troubled timeline. Upon staring the trip, I (the expedition tourist) was already operating on physiological "fumes". My personal, pre-trip complications strained my physical and cognitive state which intensified the effort of an *already* difficult task. The combined talents and agility expressed by the expedition team, enabled an experience which typically demanded 5-6 days to accomplish, in less than four days. Given our team's overall lack of conditioning and significant logistical shortfalls, I was surprised we didn't experience an event-stoppage condition.

The Tanzania natives say "Pole, Pole" (pronounced: Po-le, Po-le) in Swahili, meaning "Slow, Slow" or, one foot, in front of another. In this case, successfully ascending and descending Earth's *highest* free-standing mountain, meant we chose to stay the course, depend on each other, focus *only* on the moment, placing one foot in front of another – *Pole, Pole*. Especially when nearly exhausted – our success, purpose-oriented mindset was cemented by performing *hours* of coordinated, maximal deep breathing-while-moving measures. This approach was especially critical at times when there was "no turning back". Mindful, forward progress was the *only* option.

> "Inch by inch, step by step, '*Pole, Pole*'. Our biggest mountains are conquered with *every*, small step."
> – Conan Valente

When it comes to leading your financial and personal development journey, *Pole, Pole* may be the very approach to help you get through the challenging (or mundane) times. Personally, *Pole, Pole* enabled me to persist when the freezing weather set in (wearing shorts and a base layer shirt) and when sleep-deprived weakness completely depleted willpower. This was the first time I experienced the power of always moving, *no matter how slow*, while *inching* toward a significant achievement. Oddly enough, I "observed myself" smiling during the struggle! *Pole, Pole* saved my teammate from becoming hypoxic and quitting the trek. I witnessed *highly* conditioned guides and porters carrying supplies, who struggled to ascend the mountain; they all leveraged the secret power of *Pole, Pole* - for the *win*.

"How you do anything, is how you do everything."
– Kellie Kuecha

How we perform the little tasks, is often an indicator of how we'll perform the big challenges. If we cut corners in one aspect of our lives, we're likely to compromise other life areas, as we're only as strong as our weakest link. Mike Balboa challenges *you* to pursue personal and financial *excellence* wherever possible. In life, there are no short-cuts; only steadfast, enduring efforts of preparation, persistence, reflection, *evolution*, and *earned* realization of one's potential. How many times have we attempted to "skip steps", only to realize *all* the necessary steps are *required* to reach the goal? As with personal excellence, the *same* diligence must be applied when pursuing financial independence from real-estate investment. Effective investment and management practice execution – when performed consistently, form respective habits, over time; awaiting to yield massive, *generational* wealth. Remember, take the *all* the necessary steps, "*Pole, Pole*"; with clear, realistic goals, and vision. *Don't* let the mountain of your financial vision deter you from accepting the journey. Rather, let it serve as the *perch* of your grand-vision; visualizing and achieving *your* American Dream – the freedom and capability to *lead* the life of *your* choosing.

Since you're reading this book, you're equipped with *considerable* advantages. *You* possess the means, the will, and with *Break Rank, Make Bank, the way* to achieve financial independence with real-estate passive income. *Get after it!*

Wishing *you* and *yours* – *health and wealth*.

//Conan Valente

Introduction

Are you a junior-grade-enlisted or officer who loves the job but wishes to earn more? Have you found yourself regularly eating MREs or missing out on social activities while waiting for that paycheck on the first or fifteenth? Did you fall victim to that slick car-salesman that hoodwinked you into buying that brand-new Mustang at a 30% interest rate, but included a free tank of gas? I know the feeling. Fear not, there's still hope for you to break out of the traditional mindset and live life on your own financial terms.

This book is a resource to understand how military service can be leveraged to create monthly cash flow and true wealth through real estate investing. It is written for those currently serving (e.g., active or reserve), veterans, and potential enlistees, but also for spouses or family members who want to pass on the information to them.

The message at the core of this work is to inform you of how you can break out of the mold of "climbing up the rank ladder" and earn more money. This is not a call to disobey orders or leave the military; rather, it is a call to apply the principles in this book and have them transfer into your service to make you a better soldier, seaman, marine, airman, or even now, space guardian.

I come from a small-town, blue-collar upbringing with little education on finances or wealth accumulation. This book is inspired by the results of taking advantage of the opportunities my military service has afforded me. For me, everything changed on my first deployment when I was nineteen years old. During that period, I decided to use all my free time to read books on personal development, financial principles, and military benefits—as opposed to playing video games or spending too much time in the battlefield time machine (sleeping). When I came back to the states, I had a plan ready to implement and took immediate action in hopes of bettering my financial position in life.

Without much in the bank and zero real estate holdings, it took only four years to achieve my initial goal of $50,000 a year in net rental income, and one extra year to get to $100,000 a year—all because I started with one Veterans Affairs (VA) Loan. My goal could have been achieved even sooner, had it not been for my enrollment in a two-year training pipeline with intermittent cell phone and computer blackout dates, as well as a six-month deployment immediately afterward. The fact that I was able to stay the course and achieve those goals while living through inopportune times, demonstrates the fact that there is no excuse for you not to achieve the same or more, especially under more favorable conditions.

Those highly stressful and inopportune times were beneficial in that they forced me to systematize and automate this process after enduring a very steep learning curve. All along my journey, I kept a living document of lessons learned, tactics, techniques, and procedures that were instrumental to my success. Oftentimes, I would have to rely on others to make decisions on my behalf. Through teaching them the underlying principles to make good decisions in my absence, it validated my knowledge and efficacy of this process. It is my hope that you will be able to learn from my experiences and achieve quicker and more substantial success.

The objective of this book is to impart the knowledge on to you, so you can develop your own financial literacy that will enable you to make good decisions and take action to build your dream lifestyle through real estate investing. Once my monthly cash flow exceeded what the Army was paying me, my perception of reality changed. I no longer had to turn down weekend trips or skimp on groceries between paychecks. I could afford that new pistol and the surprising amount of ammo it took to build my skill set to be competitive in shooting matches. I now had options financially, and options create confidence and opportunities. My network continued to expand, and

I was able to learn more and do more through it. Thusly, success begat success.

I'm sharing what I have learned along the way to give my brothers and sisters in arms the knowledge to enhance their lives and take advantage of the opportunities given by the military for building true wealth. Investing in real estate is such a powerful wealth generator; and given the benefits each service member has access to, it would be turning down free money not to use them! Now, if doubling your salary sounds appealing, I implore you to heed the words written in this book and put them into action as soon as possible! Real estate investing doesn't produce millionaires overnight, but it is very rewarding to those that take consistent action.

Throughout this book we will cover exactly what the VA Loan is and how to invest with it. Additionally, you will learn how to maximize returns with your purchase, ensure profitability of your property through due diligence and cash flow analysis, manage your properties effectively, as well as how to scale and build your empire!

Why Real Estate? Real estate is a powerful investment class because it gives you more than a simple Return on Investment (ROI) percentage. For example, owning your own home allows you to receive more favorable tax treatment, such as the deduction of: modifications made to the home, the interest paid on your mortgage, property tax, and profits from home sales. In addition, with rentals you're able to earn monthly cash flow, equity, and appreciation. Furthermore, you can take advantage of the use of depreciation and leverage with your properties—which you will also learn about in this book.

- Cash flow is the term used to describe the net amount of cash going into your bank account after collecting rents and paying out expenses.
- Equity is the difference in dollars between what your home is worth and what you owe on it. Equity appreciation is achieved through the paying down of your mortgage or a higher appraised value of your home (justified by the market, home improvements, or increased rents).
- Depreciation is a powerful tool which allows you to discount the utility of the home as a whole or certain aspect of the home against your income collected from the unit. This means more in your pocket and less in Uncle Sam's.
- Leverage is possibly the most advantageous feature of investing in real estate, and this must be used correctly if you wish to fast-track yourself into managing a larger amount of assets. The first example of leverage is the amount you can finance. With a VA Loan, you can feasibly purchase a home for no cash out of pocket. This would be fully leveraging the bank to purchase your home. You may not have much equity in the property, but you

also won't spend a dime on the acquisition of an income-producing asset.

Another example of leverage would be purchasing a home at a discount price, which implies a lot of built-in equity. You'll be able to refinance or take a line of credit against the home and use that money to acquire another property. In this example, you could buy a property that needs some moderate rehab for $100,000.

Purchase Price: $100,000	80% Loan-to-Value
Down Payment: $20,000	(LTV): $128,000
Rehab Costs: $10,000	Less Mortgage: $80,000
After Rehab Value: $160,000	Cash Available: $48,000

You'll put 20% down, leveraging the bank to provide the other 80%. After putting $10,000 into rehab and repairs, the home may now appraise for $160,000. With a total investment of $30,000 ($20,000 for down payment and $10,000 for rehab), you have just created $80,000 in equity.

Lenders use a ratio called Loan-to-Value (LTV) to assess their risk in providing you a mortgage. This ratio is to determine how much you will contribute as a down-payment as well as the interest rate percentage you will pay. It's calculated by dividing the amount borrowed by the value of the property, expressed as a percentage. If the property is appraised at $100,000 and you make a $20,000 down payment, you will borrow $80,000, which is an LTV of 80%.

You will also find that the more you contribute as a down-payment, the lower interest rates you will receive as it is less of a risk to the lender. Typically, banks will lend 70–90% LTV, which means that at a conservative 80% LTV, you'll be able to pull out $48,000. You took $30,000 and turned it into $48,000, realizing a 60% return on your cash. Now, you can take those $48,000 and roll them into the purchase of another property—and snowball your way into massive wealth generation.

Oftentimes service members find themselves questioning their next career move around those ten years of service timeline. If you are only staying in ten more years for the pension, that's fine, but consider the fact that an E9 with twenty-years' time in service will draw a monthly pension of just under $4,000. With rental properties, you could surpass that amount in less than half the time. This enables you to pursue whatever it is you're truly passionate about, whether it be in or out of uniform.

Chapter 1

A PRIMER TO REAL ESTATE INVESTING

My Story: I began my real estate investing career shortly after returning from a deployment with the purchase of a 4-bedroom, 1-bathroom duplex on a college campus. I had come to the understanding that the best way to maximize my VA Loan was to purchase a multifamily unit so that I had more streams of rent coming in, as opposed to one single-family residence. With the latter, I would have to wait until I moved out to maximize the cash flow on the property. I told my realtor to only send me listings for two-to-four-unit properties, as the maximum number of dwelling units authorized under the VA Loan is four units. My intent was to live in one unit and collect the rent from the others to earn monthly cash flow. I created a spreadsheet to analyze the properties in search of one that would yield at least $500 a month in net cash flow while I was occupying it. I was considering the following: the projected rents to be collected, what the mortgage payment would be at my pre-approved interest rate, cost of homeowner's insurance, property tax, and a buffer expense (equal to 10% of total rent) for vacancies and repairs.

After analyzing over fifty properties, I finally came across one within my budget that met my criteria. It was only a duplex; but because it was considered to be on campus, the rent collected was much higher than that of similar properties outside of the campus area. One of the units had a tenant already installed and the other was vacant, so it was a perfect owner-occupant situation. Our offer included: the asking price and half of the closing costs (the other half to be covered by the seller). Since it was my first time using the VA Loan, the funding fee was only 3.3%, and I was able to wrap almost all of the remaining closing costs into my loan and only had to come up with $622 to close on the property. I "house hacked" this first property. House hacking is a way to lessen your mortgage burden or even earn income above your payment by having roommates, tenants in adjacent units, or finding other means to earn income from your property.

My friends and I lived in one half, and I rented out the other unit to a university employee. Though I wasn't charging my friends the market rate, I was paying down the mortgage, and I was even able to cash-flow over five hundred dollars into my bank account each month. That first rental check changed everything for me. I became aware of another realm of possibilities other than the traditional "go to college, get a good job, get promoted, and trade your hours for dollars until you're sixty-five" system. After that first purchase, I never looked at money the same. I had a burning desire to replace my income with money I could earn while sleeping. I gained experience in "flipping" properties: long-term single-family rentals, section 8 housing units, wholesales, multifamily units, and larger apartments.

The Five Wealth Building Principles of Real Estate Investing

Elizabeth Lizzie J. Maggie invented a game known as The Landlord's Game in 1902and patented it under her name in 1904. The intent of this game was to illustrate that "rents" enrich property owners and impoverish their tenants. She hoped that by making it into a game, it would be more digestible to a larger audience—using entertainment to educate the players in the economic impact of landownership and land valuation. Several decades later, this a similar product emerged became what is now known as the board game Monopoly by Charles B. Darrow, in which many of the Magie's original concepts and intents are still present.

Many have played this game throughout their childhood and have become none the wiser to how they could apply these concepts to their own lives and "escape the rat race." Astute observers would note, however, that owning properties and charging rent would enable them to accumulate wealth and "win the game."

Like the principles that generate wealth in Monopoly, there are principles to investing in real estate in real life that generate wealth. The way to win in Monopoly is to purchase all the properties you can. This demonstrates the value of cash flow from rent. These real-life principles are what make real estate investing such a powerful tool for wealth accumulation. I'll describe the five principles below.

Principle 1: Cash Flow. Cash flow, in the context of this book, is the amount of cash remaining after you collect rent and pay for all the expenses—such as, mortgage, tax, insurance, repairs, etc. The more rents you're able to collect and the larger the gap between rents collected and expenses paid, the more cash flow you're able to build on a monthly basis. This is the most obvious wealth builder and the most understood.

Principle 2: Appreciation of Asset. As inflation increases over the years, so does the value of the real estate asset. Typically, residential real estate assets appreciate 1–2% more than the inflation rate, all things remaining equal. You may purchase a rental property for $150,000 and without having to do any value-added work to the property, you could note that the compounding effect of the asset appreciation may raise the value of the home to $485,000 after thirty years. This is a very broad generalization of how appreciation works, not including market boom and bust cycles that can greatly impact the valuation of property. In addition to the steady increase in market appreciation, you can also force the appreciation of your asset. This can be achieved by doing value-added work to the property like modernizing the interior or exterior—also, adding features like a pool or garage.

The significance of appreciation is that it requires little input from you to widen the gap between "value of the property" and "mortgage owed" over time. You may luck out and purchase a property at the onset of a market boom and realize a 50% gain in equity from how drastically the market has appreciated. That becomes money in your pocket if you were to sell or refinance and gain access to that capital.

Principle 3: Principal Paydown. When a property is purchased using a mortgage, each monthly mortgage payment goes towards paying the loan principal and interest. Each dollar that goes towards paying down the principal becomes cash in your pocket in terms of equity that you will realize when you sell the home or refinance it. By owning a rental property (at no cost to you), your tenants are the ones providing you the cash to pay down the loan principal. Depending on how long you hold the rental, you may even find that the tenants have contributed enough rent payments to pay for your property several times over. You may be in a position where you own the property outright and have no debt to pay off when it comes time to sell. For example, you put $30,000 down on a $150,000 property. Over the life of the loan, the property has appraised to a value of $225,000, and you are not liable to pay off any debtors so in essence that $30,000 has yielded you a $195,000 return! All without having to make a single mortgage payment yourself.

Principle 4: Tax Benefits. The tax benefits associated with rental properties come in the form of deductions that will help to reduce your taxable income. The money spent on mortgage interest, insurance, repairs, and association dues is all tax deductible. You can even deduct travel and meal expenses related to the property.

Additionally, you can depreciate your rental properties every year for 27.5 years. Depreciation is a tax term which describes your ability to write off part of the value of the asset itself every year. So, each year you can write off 1/27.5 of the property's value against the income it generated. For example, if the property was purchased for $150,000, you would divide that by 27.5 to find that you can write off $5,454. If that property generates $6,000 annually in cash flow, you are only liable for the tax on $6,000 - $5,454 = $546! Imagine the savings over five, ten, twenty, or thirty rentals just like that. There are advanced strategies for larger apartments where cost segregation studies are completed for accelerated depreciation, but if you're starting out, straight-line depreciation will be the most relevant for you.

Moreover, another tax related benefit is the ability to 1031 exchange a property. A 1031 exchange is an IRS code which permits the seller of a property to reinvest its proceeds in a new property to defer all capital gains taxes. For example, you can purchase a property for $100,000 and restore it to a value of $200,000. Instead of being taxed on the profit of the proceeds when you sell the property, you can roll that amount into the purchase of a new property (within six months) and not be liable for the tax on that gain. At the time you completely exit a property without reinvesting, you will be liable for the taxes.

Finally, your classification of real estate investor can bring significant tax savings. There are three types: passive investors, active investors, and real estate professionals. You will need to work with a CPA to establish your classification, but in a nutshell, passive investors can only deduct passive losses against passive gains. This is basically saying you can only count your deductions against your rental income. Active investors can deduct up to $25,000 of their losses against other income, like a W-2 earning day job. The best classification is real estate professional, someone who completes more than 750 hours of real estate activity a year and working in the real estate industry is their primary occupation. In this instance, you can deduct all your real estate losses against your ordinary income.

Principle 5: Leverage. Real estate is possibly the easiest asset to leverage. The financing for properties usually offers the lowest interest rates of all loan products. At the time of writing this book, interest rates are below 3% and the loans are routinely amortized over 30-year periods. Additionally, you pay at most 20–25% down payments for these properties. With the right strategy and implementation, you can purchase real estate, improve its value, then refinance out of it to recover 100% or more of your capital. You're taking money from a bank and paying it back with money from a tenant and keeping the difference for yourself.

Check on Learning:

The Five Wealth Building Principles of Real Estate:

- Cash Flow

- Asset Appreciation

- Principal Paydown

- Tax Benefits

- Leverage

Chapter 2

YOUR VA LOAN ADVANTAGE

So, what is the VA Loan? The VA Loan is a loan product only for individuals with VA entitlement. Straight from the VA Benefits Home Loan web page, it states that: "VA Home Loans are provided by private lenders, such as banks and mortgage companies. VA guarantees a portion of the loan, enabling the lender to provide you with more favorable terms." This means that if you qualify for the VA Loan, you're able to secure better interest rates, loan terms, and possibly closing fees because the VA guarantees up to 25% of the loan, which means it's less risky for the banks. Additionally, there is no longer a limit on how much you can borrow through a VA Loan, it is simply the maximum amount the lender determines you can qualify for. Moreover, the lenders will not discriminate if you have a history of bankruptcy or foreclosure, you can still secure a VA Loan.

There are two VA Loan products. The conventional loan and the construction loan. The conventional loan is what you're more familiar with in that it is the loan used to purchase a primary residence with as little as no money down for one to four dwelling units. Five units or more are considered commercial class property, and the VA Home Loan cannot be used for those purchases. The VA Construction Loan is also a no money down loan; but to use this product, banks typically require you to have already purchased the land you intend to build on, then they will loan you the construction costs or allow you to refinance the entire project into a VA Loan upon completion.

What makes this loan so special is your ability to purchase a home with essentially no money out of pocket due to the ability to wrap closing costs, funding fees, and still receive the lowest interest rates. Also, no Private Mortgage Insurance (PMI) is needed either. Most lenders require 20% down to avoid paying the monthly PMI. Though you won't pay PMI, there is a VA funding fee which can be paid upfront or wrapped into the loan. For example, with my first purchase, the home was listed for $315,000 and I wrapped my funding fee of $3,000 into the loan. The amount varies depending on your down payment amount, number of times using the loan, and if you have any service-connected disabilities. Veterans with a disability rating are exempt from the funding fee.

The VA charges a funding fee to help protect themselves from those that default on their mortgages. The fees range from 0.5% to 3.3% of the loan amount, however, your lender can wrap that fee into your loan if you do not want to pay out of pocket for it. Also, if you have any VA disability rating, you can receive exemption from this fee.

For example, on a $300,000 home, the fee could range from $1,500 to $9,900. Typically, for your first purchase, you will pay the 0.5% and subsequent loan uses will warrant a higher percentage unless you have a disability rating. I was charged 0.5% in my first use of the VA Loan and the full 3.3% for my second use. The second time around (a property worth $495,000), it only amounted to a difference in my payments of fifty-five dollars more a month. In most situations, I advise to wrap it into the loan because $10,000 amortized over 30 years hurts much less than going into your freezer, gun safe, or mattress and pulling out $10,000 in cold, hard cash—and physically feeling it slip through your fingertips.

Who Is Eligible? You must be a veteran or actively serving, with intent to occupy the property as a home within a reasonable time frame after closing the loan. You'll need to qualify as a satisfactory credit risk, and your income must show to be stable and enough to meet the mortgage payments while having enough left over for life expenses.

The first thing you should do is log on to Credit Karma, or any other secure credit score website, and find out what your credit score is. You'll want to go over all the factors that impact your credit score and make some phone calls to clear up any discrepancies.

The point is to make sure there is an accurate representation of your credit and spending history. Keep in mind, there are hard and soft credit inquiries. A soft inquiry is when you check your own credit score through Credit Karma, or your credit card company, and this does not impact your credit score. A hard inquiry is when a bank reviews your credit as part of their decision-making process. This inquiry typically lowers your credit score for a short period. Looking on your own will save your score in the event you find it to be already too low. You won't prompt a hard inquiry and receive a credit ding only to find out you are unable to get the loan.

 Bank-on-it Tip #1:

When it comes time to shop for a lender, do your due diligence and research potential lenders, whether they be national or local institutions. You can apply for credit with several lenders at once. Multiple credit inquiries close together will not do as much damage to your score as they will if they are spaced weeks or months apart. Your lender will have the visibility to see why your credit has been pulled in the past and use their judgment to see if you have dings from shopping around, not due to high credit utilization or missed payments.

The VA Loan doesn't require a minimum credit score. Banks can work with you on a case-by-case basis. However, your best bet is to work with a lending agent that specializes in the VA Loan, or a bank that produces a high volume of VA Loans—so they are best able to advise you on your specific situation and financial needs. From what I am currently seeing in the field as of this writing, most home buyers with a credit score of 620 or higher can close on a home without issue and still receive favorable interest rates.

As an aside, the amount of experience in processing VA Loans your lender has correlates to the amount of stress you will face in closing on your deal. Remember, the loan originator is a salesman. Their job is to get you to borrow their bank's money. The processor and underwriter are the gatekeepers. They're the ones you will have all your last-minute, uncannily inconvenient immediate suspense emails with and even sometimes forced to leave a restaurant early to scan and submit documents!

How to become more eligible. The more income you earn, the less debt you have, and the higher your credit score is—which will ultimately lead you to the best financing terms and conditions.

Tips to improve your credit score include:

Tip 1: Lowering your Debt-to-Income (DTI) ratio percentage.

The Debt-to-Income (DTI) ratio is a measure that compares your monthly debt payment to your monthly gross income. To calculate your DTI, simply divide your total monthly debt by your gross monthly income like so:

DTI = (Total Monthly Debt) / (Gross Monthly Income)
Multiply that decimal result by 100 to achieve your percentage.

(DTI) x (100) = %
Most banks want you to have a DTI of less than 45%. However, I have seen friends approved with a 55% DTI when they were buying a multifamily with tenants actively paying rent at the time of purchase.

Tip 2: Take advantage of service member protection against extreme interest rates.

As exampled in the introduction, if you were one of the inevitable many who purchased, say, a brand-new Camaro the day you got out of basic training at a 32% interest rate plus a free tank of gas, fear not. The reason I bring this up is because there are laws enacted to protect service members against extreme interest rates. You simply need to make a quick Google search for whatever you currently have high interest rates on (credit cards, auto loans, personal loans, etc.), find the policy or regulation that covers that product, and renegotiate with your loan provider.

For example, under the Service Member Civil Relief Act (SCRA), credit card companies are unable to levy an interest rate higher than 6% a year on service members. Give your credit card company a call today if you haven't already signed up for this! If you have paid more than that, they are liable to retroactively reimburse you for interest exceeding 6%.

A few other tips to help boost your credit score include:

- Pay your bills on time.
- Get credit for making utility and cell phone payments on time.
- Check out Experian Boost (free online) which allows you to connect your bank accounts to identify utility and cellphone payment history. After verification, it adds that record to your FICO score.
- Maintain a low utilization rate. If your total credit limit is $10,000, try to keep your monthly credit spending below $3,000.
- Only apply for new credit accounts as needed to avoid unnecessary credit inquiries. However, each time you do get a new line of credit or loan, it brings down the average age of your credit history. Lenders like to see a long history of on-time

payments. For that same reason, don't close old or unused credit cards unless they charge you an annual fee.

Here are the areas to work on in order to prepare yourself to be the ideal applicant:

Credit Score. Banks are going to do what is known as a "hard pull" on your credit. Monitoring your FICO score through your credit card company is great; however, the bank utilizes three different agencies and selects the lowest score—which could be as much as a 50pt swing from what you see on FICO. Do what you can to get your credit score as high as possible; check out Credit Karma online and run your credit through them. They give you a free analysis of how to improve your score. Factors that attribute to your score: length of credit history, history of on-time payments, history of no missed payments, no current accounts in collections, multiple credit accounts, and low usage of credit limits.

Income. Banks love the fact that you get paid on the first and fifteenth of every month. However, as an enlisted service member, you're not exactly crushing it when it comes to income. This is where having a side job or hustle that you document on your taxes can really help your position. Also, if you are married and both spouses work, this will be more appealing to the banks as well. They typically ask for the tax returns of the last two years; so, in the case where you work a cash job on the side (e.g., waitering), think about if it would be worth it to report a 1099 or claim the tips you earn—because it could make the difference between you landing a larger deal or not.

Cash Reserves. Having a large cash reserve will bring your lender to trust you more as it demonstrates you can continue payments in the event of an emergency or job transition. The more cash you have in the bank after expected closing costs, the more comfortable a lender will be with you. Since when is having too much cash ever a bad thing, right?

Co-borrower. I don't typically recommend this option as it opens the door to a lot of complications, potential headaches, or loss down the road—but it is an option if you are unable to secure a loan on your own. If you are married to or trust another person with VA eligibility, they can become a co-borrower and you could still receive the VA guarantee. Persons without VA eligibility would not receive VA guarantee for their portion of the loan. Just keep in mind, you're establishing a relationship with this person for the life of your loan or until you can refinance them out of it. If you're anything like me and can't even commit to the same scent of deodorant, imagine what can change between two people within thirty years of a loan!

Chapter 3

LENDER SHOPPING

How to Shop for a Reputable Lender. There are many nuances involved with the VA Loan, and each loan applicant will face a different scenario that may cause some difficulties throughout the process. For this reason, working with someone who is experienced in VA lending and has completed many of these loans can hopefully prevent the death of a deal. This type of lender will be able to foresee problems and know the best way to present your application to the underwriter for loan approval.

Many times, your real estate agent will give you a referral to a bank for you to use. Be wary of this because oftentimes they'll receive a kickback of some sort, so just be sure to do your due diligence and shop multiple credit unions and banks (local and national). Also, vet the lender with questions such as:

- How many VA Loans have you processed?
- What are the fees associated with using your bank?

- What are the current VA requirements for loans (credit score, debt-to-income ratio, etc.)?
- How long does it take your bank to close these types of loans?
- Have you recently done deals in the area where the property is located?
- Have you recently used appraisers in the property area and what was your experience with them like?

Additionally, you should evaluate how the banker operates. Is the lender easy to get a hold of and responsive? If they are nonresponsive and take a long time to get back to you, it may be in your best interest to find someone else to work with.

Working with a bad agent can be overcome if the bank at least has some perks that you're unable to find elsewhere. Some benefits could include:

- Lowest interest rates.
- Lowest bank and closing fees.
- Not selling off your mortgage (keeping it in-house).
- Possibility for cash back at closing
- No prepayment penalties.
- Shorter period before you can refinance.
- Favorable refinancing terms.
- A good online or mobile app platform with remote deposit availability.

- Other services that you may want to take advantage of—such as, bundling your home insurance, auto insurance, and motorcycle insurance with them to save on all three.

Saving Money Along the Way. There are various ways in which you can continue to save money on the way to building your real estate empire.

Saving on down payments. The number one benefit of using a VA Loan is the fact that you may be able to purchase a home with literally no money out of your own pocket. For the first home I purchased, I only had to come up with $622—not bad for a $320,000 duplex. Take note, however, that your monthly payments are going to be higher with a 0% down payment as opposed to a 20% down payment. In this deal, I only had to come up with $622 instead of $64,000.

The difference was paying a $1,459 mortgage as opposed to a $1,168 mortgage. This meant that there was a potential to earn $291 more in my pocket per month had I gone with a higher down payment. The property still produced over $1,500 a month in net cash flow at 0% down, so I still considered it an obvious win. Your priority with this purchase is to make cash flow each month, so if it isn't possible with no money down, you may want to find another deal. You could also increase the purchase price to get sellers to assist in closing costs or increase the amount you contribute as down payment to make your numbers work.

 Bank-on-it Tip #2:

Given a 4% interest rate, every $10,000 you increase or decrease in loan principle only raises or lowers your monthly payment by forty-eight dollars. So, don't be intimidated by a few thousand dollars when negotiating a sale price.

Saving on Private Mortgage Insurance (PMI). Another key feature savings is the fact that there is no Private Mortgage Insurance (PMI) with VA Loans. PMI is what lenders charge borrowers when a mortgage is taken out with a down payment of less than 20%. This is a monthly savings that comes to you at no additional cost. PMI oftentimes costs between 0.5% and 1% of the loan amount per year. So, if you have a $300,000 home, you're saving an extra $250 a month: $3,000 a year.

Also, borrowers of the VA Loan are not required to pay duplicate fees for services already paid for by previous prospective purchasers. For example, if an appraisal was completed on a property but the deal fell through and now you are in contract with the home, you are not subject to pay for a new appraisal if you are within the time window of a valid Notice of Value (NOV). Typically, a NOV is valid for six months. Home appraisals usually cost within $300 to $400 for single families—but as you get into multifamily units, the price could reach upwards of $1,000.

Getting loan quotes from multiple lenders. You may find that certain banks charge much higher origination fees, document preparation fees, or even membership fees. Try at least three different banks and a credit union to compare their total costs to close on the home. You may find that you can save a couple thousand dollars depending on the purchase price. Most often, you will find that credit unions will have the lowest closing costs, followed by the local banks, then national chains.

Also, you can meet with the lender in person or over the phone to talk about your financial situation before they go ahead and pull your credit. This may save you a credit ding and provide you with a knowledgeable source for advice. Talking with them and building a good rapport may enable you to work together to find ways to make the deal work, whereas you may've gotten a flat out "no" from another bank that was more transactional.

Time of year. Typically, spring and summer demand the highest prices for homes, and if you're able to time it right, you may save between 10–20% of the sale price by purchasing in the winter months.

Negotiation with seller. Oftentimes, you can increase the purchase price and negotiate with the seller to pay anywhere from some to all of your closing costs, and they will structure it to net them the same amount of profit as they would have received from the original sale price. This happened on a triplex for me. I was able to work with the seller to increase the sale price of the home so that I could get cash to pay off credit cards at closing. The home was listed for $395,000 and we agreed upon a sale price of $415,000 with a net to seller amount of $390,000.

This meant that $15,000 were available to cover the closing costs. Since there was an additional $6,000 left over after paying the closing costs, I was able to use that amount for paying down credit card debt. Actually, the VA requires any additional funds be used to pay off existing consumer debt before straight up cash is given to you at closing.

It's important to note that in order to do this kind of negotiation, the property must appraise for near the price you agree upon and if the purchase price is above the appraised value, you may be asked to come up with 25% of the difference as cash to close. Also, most other lenders will give you the remaining amount back as cash to you at closing.

VA Loan Requirements and Hurdles. Minimum Property Requirements (MPR) may be a deal killer. The VA is very strict about the condition of the homes you're allowed to buy with this loan product. You most likely will not be able to buy a full scope fixer-upper with this loan. Meaning, you can buy a property that does need some repairs and still turn it for profit, but the typical repairs required in a total "fix and flip" scenario would be outside of the MPR. The objective of the MPR is to make sure the buyer is getting a home that is safe, structurally sound, and sanitary. While that may seem like a large generalization, the VA appraisers are the final say in the appropriateness of the home.

According to the Lenders Handbook – VA Pamphlet 26-7 (<u>Chapter 12 Minimum Property Requirement</u>, some of the requirements are as follows:

- The property must be promptly vendible (easily resold).
- The property must be big enough for the inhabitants to live, sleep, cook, and eat in with sanitary facilities.
- The property must be compliant with local building codes.
- The property must have an easy entrance for a vehicle or a pedestrian year-round, with legal access to gain entrance to the property (no easements; or if there is a shared private road, there should be an enforceable agreement on who pays for maintenance).

- There should be no encroachments on the home. (a neighbor's roof, fence, garage, or other, may not cross over your property line).
- Waste and surface water must flow off the property quickly and positively, not forming ponds.
- The property must be free from any geological risk (e.g., a mudslide, sinkhole, or gradual cave-in of land).
- The property should be located away from flood zones (if the home cannot be insured against flood hazards, the VA will not guarantee your loan).
- The property must be used mainly as a residence (cannot be zoned commercial unless the township authorizes residential use of the property).
- The property must be supplied with electricity to provide lighting and operate needed appliances (any damaged or dangerous wiring must be fixed before receiving loan approval).
- Utilities must not be interrupted by neighboring land or services (there must be access for contractors to get to your utilities to maintain and repair them without any interference from neighboring land or buildings; multiunit homes must have their own service shutoffs).
- The property must have a regular water supply that is potable and have a secure discard of sewage.
- The property cannot have construction defects, poor workmanship, continuing settlement under foundation, too much dampness, leaks, decay, or

termite infestation (these issues must be addressed prior to receiving the loan).

- If installed, the property must have operational heating and air-conditioning.
- The property must not have leaks or decay in the roof.
- The property must not have dampness in the basement (if a sump pump is installed, it must be safely hardwired or plugged into a standard electrical outlet).
- If the property has an operational swimming pool, it must meet local code.
- If the property is fitted with burglar bars, each bedroom must have a quick-release mechanism on at least one window.
- The property must not have any lead-based paint.
- The property must not pose any environmental hazards: oil and gas wells, underground storage tanks, chemical contamination, slush pits, soil contamination from sources on or off the property, or hydrogen sulfide gas from petroleum product wells.
- The property cannot be built in a Clear Zone or Runway Protection Zone for airports because it would be too close to an active runway.
- If the property is a manufactured mobile home, it must have a foundation that can bear the weight of the home and resist strong winds, conform with local and state regulations, and a floor area of at

least 400 square feet if it's a singlewide or 700 square feet if it's a double wide.
- Modular homes are acceptable.

The appraisal the VA conducts on the property is like a soft inspection. It's very detailed and they are generally looking out for your best interest. Be aware, you may find the appraiser to show concern over certain things in the home that do not bother you at all or that you would have even overlooked.

They can create a situation in which they determine the property doesn't align with the MPR and cause a complication in your deal—requiring the seller to resolve the issue before closing or for you to resolve it within a short period after closing. However, you can waive your right to a home inspection (accepting the property as it is) to make a deal using the VA Loan. This can help in strengthening your offer on the property because sellers appreciate the "less hassle" that comes from buying a property as-is. Knowing that the VA appraiser will be doing a thorough job in their walk-through of the home will give you confidence that they may catch something significant you overlooked in your own walk-through, and you can use that for negotiation leverage.

Then again, appraisals become more of a concern with multifamily units as you're hoping for them to arrive at the same valuation as your purchase price. Oftentimes, multifamily units are valued based upon their rental income and not necessarily the comparable value of similar homes in the area. For example, I tried buying a duplex in another college town which was listed for $800,000. The property collected just under $8,000 a month in rent because it charged by the room to college students. Unfortunately, there was a home of similar construction down the block which was not used as a college rental and had recently sold for $245,000. The VA appraiser was unable to give the property the $800,000 valuation based on their methods of comparable sales or cost approach, and the income approach couldn't reflect the full rent collection because it would be considered an owner-occupant home.

This is one of the reasons why in a hot market, seller agents are hesitant to work with buyers using a VA Loan. They know that VA lending is tied more to the appraisal of the home than the agreed upon sale price. If the market is hot and the VA appraiser doesn't come close to the sale price, the VA buyer typically backs out of the deal. Additionally, the length of time to process a VA Loan is greater than that of the conventional loans. Forty-five days is typically standard for VA Loans whereas the conventional loan standard is thirty days. Buyers looking to collect their cash quickly may choose to exclude VA buyers if they have plenty of offers to choose from. It's been my observation that if a house goes on the market and within a week is already asking for highest and best offers, VA Loan buyers are typically not as competitive. Conventional loans allow for more flexibility in deal structure in this environment. Don't be discouraged, it is a challenge to perseverance and patience and if you are applying consistent effort, you will secure a victory.

Check on Learning:

1. How can you find a reputable lender?

- Compile a list of potential lenders from Google and call each one to vet them.

- Decide the pros and cons of working with each and choose the one you feel best meets   your criteria.

2. What are some ways to save money when purchasing a home?

- Utilize the "No Money Down" aspect of the VA Loan.

- Get multiple loan estimates from lenders.

- Negotiate with the seller.

- Consider the time of year or market phase.

3. What considerations must you be mindful of when utilizing a VA Loan?

- Minimum Property Requirements as dictated in the VA Lenders Pamphlet.

Chapter 4

INCOME INCREASING STRATEGIES

In this chapter, we will cover the ways of maximizing your Basic Allowance for Housing (BAH) and rental income. There are several strategies listed below, but your only limit is how far your creativity can go. The goal is to find ways to earn enough income to not have to pay a mortgage, or better yet, earn more than you need to spend monthly on your mortgage.

House Hacking. Simply put, "house hacking" is finding a way to earn income that offsets your out-of-pocket cost of paying your mortgage. A few examples could be:

- Leasing out rooms individually.
- Creating separate living spaces and converting your single-family home into a multifamily.
- Renting rooms out on Airbnb.
- Purchasing a multifamily unit where you live in one unit and rent out the other one/two/three.
- Hosting a foreign exchange student or fostering children.

- Renting out garage space or land.
- Creating an apartment in your garage.
- Building a guest house / trailer.
- Becoming a "registered agent" for small businesses.

Below are some descriptions of a few of these examples.

Example 1: Rent Out Rooms

For example, say you have a $180,000 3-bedroom, 2-bathroom home with a total mortgage, insurance, and tax payment of $945 a month. You're an E5 at Fort Bragg earning $1,233 a month in BAH. Instantly, you're able to save $288 a month towards your next rental. However, you want to build that savings even faster and decide to house hack. You're able to find some roommates and rent out the other two rooms at a rate of $500 per room. Now, you're collecting $1,000 a month from rental income, fifty-five dollars over your mortgage payment! You're able to save your entire BAH allowance, a tax-free annual amount of $14,796. Simply renting out the other two rooms took you from being able to save $3,456 a year to $14,796! This is a great practice for service members because BAH is a tax-free pay, and the rental income is not taxable as long as you are also using it as your primary residence—and not technically profiting from it. In this example, the fifty-five dollars a month translates to $660 for the year that can easily be offset by costs related to maintaining the property, advertising, insurance, Homeowners' Association (HOA) fees, utilities, or mortgage interest.

People have varying opinions as to whether they should claim rental income on their taxes or not—since there's very little likelihood the IRS is going to come searching for your one property with roommates. To determine what's best for your situation, consider your goals. If you are wanting to grow into a reputable organization with a large portfolio, it's in your best interest to abide by the law and claim the taxes. It's worth noting that real estate is one of the best means to shelter taxes, so just because you're going to claim the income, doesn't necessarily mean you will be forced to pay the taxman.

There are many advanced strategies that are beyond the scope of this book, but I also recommend you hire an experienced certified public accountant, for they will steer you in the right direction. One thing to know is that banks—when looking at your financial statement—typically want to see a two-year rental history for them to be able to include the rental income from a property as part of your total earned income. I claim my rental incomes immediately because it adds credibility when I go loan shopping. It shows that I have a paper trail history of landlording and earning rental income.

By claiming the income from the year I purchase the property, I'm essentially a year ahead of the curve since I have one year of landlording and collecting rent as a track record—even though I'm living at the property. When I move out the next year and the property shows the cash flow from being fully rented, the lender will work with me on using that income because I've already been managing the property for two years. Lenders may have some questions for you down the road if you've never claimed your income from ten properties on your taxes, and you're telling the lenders that they produce $50,000 a year in income. In Example 1, the taxes you would owe on $660 is negligible anyway.

Example 2: Creating Living Spaces (Basement Apartment)

Creating a separate living space or a basement apartment could be very easily done by you or—without too high of a price tag—by a contractor, depending on the layout of your home. If you have a layout that could easily permit separate or private access to a couple hundred square feet of living space, you can hire a contractor to install the necessary modifications to the space. You can enable it to have a separate kitchen, bathroom, and bedroom where you can either live in that part and rent out the larger portion of your home or vice versa. This is nice because you've created two completely separate living spaces and won't have to worry about all of the issues roommates bring up. When you go away for deployments or training, you can just lock it all up and have less concerns about sticky-fingered tenants.

Example 3: Multifamily Home

Purchasing a multifamily is what I personally believe to be the most advantageous use of the VA Loan. I recommend a college town or a location that demands rents that are higher than 1% of the purchase price of the home. For example, let's say you purchase a $300,000 triplex with a $1,530 a month mortgage, tax, and insurance payment and that the market rents are $1,500 per unit—you will be able to cover your mortgage with one unit rented. Then, you can cash-flow $1,500 with two units rented. Finally, when you move out and rent out all three, you'll be cash-flowing $3,000! That's an amazing return on your investment if you were able to purchase the home for almost no money down.

Example 4: Work as a Registered Agent

Landlords and other small businesses will use this service if, for example, the township where they have their rentals or business in requires the owner to live within a certain radius of their business or rental property. If the owner does not have an address within those confines, they must hire a property manager or registered agent. A registered agent for an LLC is an agent for "service of process" as well as receiving other correspondence on behalf of the LLC.

The agent must forward these materials to the LLC in a timely manner. So basically, you just need to have an address that is not a PO Box, and when you receive mail specific to the LLC you're representing, you forward it to them at their actual address. If you or a spouse don't travel very often, this could be a very good opportunity for you. Typically, registered agents cost between $100–$500 a year (depending on their services), so if you're looking at this route, you may want to consider doing some marketing to make it worthwhile. Additionally, you could get certified as a notary and realize some income from that as well.

Maximizing Your BAH. If you're in the National Guard or Reserves, this section will be more applicable to you as you have much more freedom in your ability to relocate. The first thing I would do is go online to look up the states that interest you and scroll through their zip codes to see which pay the highest BAH. You can find the 2021 BAH Rates By State and Local MHA page in the MilitaryBenefits.info website.

After you find the state, you've been wanting to move to and find the highest BAH rates, you can either transfer to serve in that state or update your home of record to reflect that zip code with your current unit.

The most advantageous thing about serving in the Guard or Reserves is the fact that your BAH entitlement is based on your home of record, not the base from which you drill. Below are some of the highest paying BAH stipends based on E-5 with dependents:

- San Francisco, CA = $4,398
- New York, NY = $3,378
- Boston, MA = $3,075
- New Haven, CT = $2,901
- Seattle, WA = $2,574
- Ft. Lauderdale, FL = $2,547

If you're able to find a room to rent or even a cheap home to buy within the San Francisco BAH area, you'll be making just under $40,000 of tax-free income on a nine-month deployment from BAH alone. You'll want to have a lease agreement, civilian job pay stubs, mortgage payment records, a utility bill, credit card transaction records, or something in your name showing that you live there so as not to commit BAH fraud. This could be a very viable method to substantially increase your income if you're not bound to living in any certain location. If it's something that you are interested in, you could volunteer for deployments or Temporary Duty Travel (TDY) training so as to make it worth the hassle of moving to get all that extra BAH pay.

The next thing I would check before committing to a move is if the state gives any income tax exemptions to military pay. Some only exempt combat zone pays while deployed, others exempt any service pay. To name a few states that exempt service and retirement pay:

Arkansas	Maine	New York
Alabama	Massachusetts	North Dakota
Connecticut	Michigan	Ohio
Hawaii	Minnesota	Pennsylvania
Illinois	Mississippi	Vermont
Iowa	Missouri	Virginia
Kansas	Montana	West Virginia
Louisiana	New Jersey	Wisconsin

You'll want to do your own research to confirm, as each year laws are subject to change.

Another thing to keep in mind is the fact that the BAH rates in those top locations are high for a reason, the cost of living. You may come to realize that investing in those areas is a strategy that would not be profitable for you. If this is the case, you may try to hop on a couple deployments with that state to save up and reach a certain goal, then transfer back to an area where you're more familiar with its housing market. You can also invest long-distance if you have a team or network in place at your desired investing location. I bring this topic up because many in the Guard or Reserves are single and oftentimes do not have a very high-paying civilian job set up, or they are not maximizing their ability to make money with the military—so it's good to explore these options. Being flexible with where you hang your hat can really pay dividends.

If you're on active duty, you don't have nearly as much say in where you live. One thing to keep in mind is that most landlords in military towns know what the BAH rate is and typically market their properties accordingly. On one end of the spectrum, it's frustrating to be a renter in this type of environment, but on the other end of the spectrum—when you're the one offering a rental—you can make much smarter purchases since you already have a pretty concrete understanding of what the market rate will bear. This enables you to feel more confident about your cash flow predictions before making your purchase.

An example of the buying power difference in BAH rate between states and what they can give you:
Let's say you're an E5 without dependents, earning BAH, and stationed in Fort Campbell, Kentucky. Your BAH rate is $1,245. Assuming you put 0% down, your interest rate is 3.5% amortized over 30 years, and escrowed taxes and insurance amounting to $250 a month for a total payment of $1,227 per month. You could buy a $220,000 home and have eighteen dollars

remaining from your BAH allowance. On the flipside, there may be a duty position you can fill located in Key West, Florida. The E5 (without dependent) BAH there is $2,334. Assuming 0% down, an interest rate of 3.5% amortized over 30 years, and escrowed taxes and insurance amounting to $375 a month for a total payment of $2,283 per month.

You could buy a $425,000 home and have fifty-one dollars remaining from your BAH allowance. Most likely, you don't need all the house that a $425,000 single-family home would provide you, but maybe that price range will get you a nice cash-flowing multifamily property. This is just an example to spark some thought generation.

In the above example, there are opportunities in both markets to purchase a great cash-flowing property. However, due to your increase of pay and property values in the Key West market, you may find that you're more easily able to get into approved for a 3- or 4-unit multifamily home with higher purchasing power as well as income generated from the other units. Keep in mind that you are building equity each month the mortgage is being paid down. If the tenants are completely covering your mortgage, you're essentially having them not only make your mortgage payments but also indirectly pay you via the equity accrued in your home. Once that $425,000 Key West home is paid off and continued to be used as a rental, that's an extra $2,000 coming into your bank account each month that you did zero work to earn. Or better yet, you can utilize a line of credit or a cash-out refinance to expedite your purchase power and timeline.

Let's look at this table to show the power of loan paydown and equity appreciation for that $425,000 home.

Time	Home Value	Loan Pay Down	Equity $
After 5 yrs	$469,234	$88,819	$133,053
After 10 yrs	$518,072	$96,885	$189,957
After 15 yrs	$571,994	$159,172	$306,166
After 20 yrs	$631,527	$233,352	$439,879
After 25 yrs	$697,257	$321,696	$593,953
After 30 yrs	$769,828	$425,000	$769,828

These numbers are powerful. Take a minute to think about the wealth that buying a home with your VA Loan can create. In this example, you bought a $425,000 home in Key West, Florida, at 3.5% interest rate, amortized over 30 years. Immediately you begin collecting rent, and this table shows the value of appreciation potential of that home. It doesn't even include the cash flow you would have accumulated over all this time! Assuming a consistent inflation level of appreciation in the home value over the course of 30 years, your $425,000 property will be worth three-quarters of a million dollars. You haven't had to pay a cent towards the mortgage because you've had it filled with tenants each year. The tenants are paying off your home and while you're accumulating equity, the appreciation is rising and now you have a compounding effect of wealth generation!

An investment such as this opens so many doors for you to scale up and grow your investment portfolio. After year 5 (according to the table above), you could take out a line of credit against the home for $100,000 and use that money for down payments on several single-family homes, a smaller multifamily home, an apartment, or a business venture you've been dreaming of. From here on out, the investment income you're earning begins to snowball and it's off to the races to achieve your financial independence number.

21 Tips for Building Up Cash

The abovementioned means to getting into your next deal are tried and true methods with successful track records. If you're in between phases and noticing you need to get together some extra cash on top of what you're able to save from your job, below is a list of side hustles for some thought generation. The sky is the limit for where your creativity and hard work can take you. I simply offer these as mere suggestions to get your mind warmed up and thinking about what you could do to place yourself in the direction of generating income from properties.

1) Take a loan from your Thrift Savings Plan (TSP) or 401(k) retirement account.
2) Take a loan from your whole life insurance policy.
3) Utilize 0% APR credit card terms to pay yourself the limit.
4) Set up an Etsy business.
5) Resell on Amazon/eBay/craigslist/Facebook marketplace.
6) Drive Uber or Lyft.
7) Pet-sit or babysit.
8) Become an online tutor or virtual assistant.
9) Airbnb your home or a friend's home.
10) Rent your car or motorcycle with apps like Toro or in websites like Riders Share.
11) Go to garage and yard sales, purchase items, and resell them.
12) Open a new bank account for introductory offers (between $100–$500).
13) Find ways to monetize a skill set, passion, or hobby you have online.
14) Try income-generating apps: Swagbucks, InboxDollars, Rakuten, Instacart, Survey Junkie.
15) Look on craigslist or local postings for random jobs you can do.
16) Take on a part-time job.

17) Put together events and charge for admission or sponsorship.

18) Sell food or baked goods.

19) Arbitrage: find anything at a discount and sell it for a profit.

20) Give blood plasma.

21) Google how to earn extra money!

 Bank-on-it Tip #3:

A quick note on the TSP retirement investment program mentioned in the list above. If you are a reservist working full-time for a 401(k)-sponsoring employer that matches employee contribution, you can continue to fund that 401(k) and roll it over to the TSP at any time. The TSP will then consider the transfer to be all "employee contribution"—including what your employer contributed. So, if your employer has been contributing 6% for years, you will now have access to that chunk of money and can take out a loan from your TSP. You can only borrow "employee contributions" so that's a creative way to circumvent the rule and create more wealth for yourself. The terms of payback are very favorable, and the interest rate is much lower than borrowing from a traditional 401(k). It can act like a revolving line of credit; once you pay off your loan, you are only required to wait sixty days to borrow from it again.

Check on Learning:

1. What are some methods to increase your income?

- House Hack.

- Maximize your BAH.

- Refer to the 21 tips for building up cash.

2. What should your mindset be?

- Ask yourself, "How can I afford this?" instead of saying "I can't afford this."

Chapter 5

DUE DILIGENCE

What is due diligence? The first step in your journey to purchasing a rental home should include a market analysis. You want to know all the important factors that will enable you to make a good decision about the area. The "market cycle" phase you are in and the implications of local laws, tax structure, rent rates, environmental impact, and future forecast can make or break a deal for you—the savvy investor. The more planning you can do with the "end in mind," the higher your likelihood of success will be. Sure, you can get away with blindly purchasing a home and possibly having the numbers work out, but for sustainable and repeatable success, you must have a process or system in place that is a model for achieving your goals.

I like to use a top-down approach when considering a new market. I'll walk you through it now. Firstly, give yourself a mind-set check. How would purchasing this property affect your present situation a year from now, three years from now, five years from now?

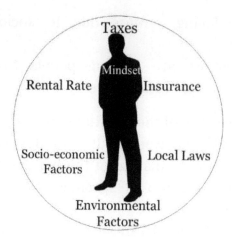

For example, are you looking to purchase a home this year and are also planning to attend a selection to another career field—that may require a Permanent Change of Station (PCS)—next year?

Ask yourself the following questions to help yourself think into the future:

- How will that affect the way you manage the property and the way it cash-flows?
- How about five years from now?
- Will the property increase in value?
- Are there repairs you intend to do that would justify an increase in value?
- Does the area seem to be increasing in population and economic demand—or is it decreasing?
- Does it seem likely rents would remain constant, will they bear increases tied to inflationary costs, or is there a likelihood they could decrease as the

area is losing renters due to socioeconomic factors?

- What factors are causing people to leave or bringing people into the area?

These are some of the questions that you should be able to quickly answer about your desired market. After satisfactorily answering the big questions, you should then delve into the specifics of the area you're considering.

The Four Market Phases. There are four phases to a market cycle, consisting of two opportune times to sell and two opportune times to buy.

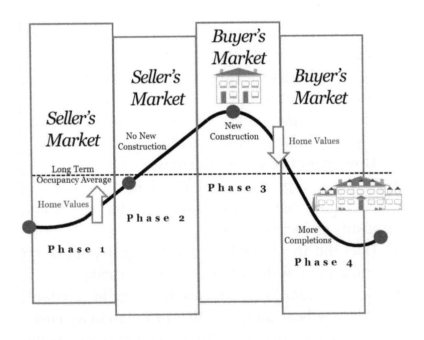

At any point in a market, you can observe statistics related to construction, employment, number of households, household income, vacancy rates, and rental rates to determine which phase you are in.

Phase 1: Home values are increasing due to increase of demand. The increase in home values may be reflective of large employment coming to an area, an incentive for people to migrate to this location, or simply the timing of the market. Indicators of this market include:

- Decreasing supply of homes on the market.
- Short time on market.
- Low unemployment.
- Increasing home values and rent rates.
- Strong demand for properties.

You'll want to be careful in your property analysis during this phase because you will be losing out on long-term appreciation. No one will be able to predict just how high the market will increase, so be very conservative in your underwriting. Look for properties with good cash flow or deals where you could achieve a quicker entry and exit from to capitalize on selling at the top of a seller's market.

Phase 2. Supply is increasing due to increase in new construction and sellers wanting to capitalize on the appreciation of home values. Demand is strong, however, there isn't quite the excess of a supply to generate a buyer's market. Indicators of this market include:

- Longer time on market.
- Increasing supply of homes on the market.
- Home prices still inflated.
- Increasing demand and costs for construction and material.
- Slowing job growth.

This is the time to sell. You're recognizing the indicators that you are reaching a top of the market and any properties you are looking to exit soon should be listed at this time. If you're wanting to shield yourself from taxes, look to 1031 and into a strong cash-flowing asset. Otherwise, hold on to the property and increase your cash until the opportune time in a buyer's market phase comes along.

Phase 3. There's an oversupply of inventory in the market. An oversupply of inventory may be the cause of a very hot market that is no longer booming, and the construction exceeded the demand. Indicators that you are in this phase include:

- Decreasing home values, possible rent decreases as well.
- Longer time on the market.
- Increasing unemployment numbers.
- Increasing bank foreclosures.

In this phase, you are amidst the decline of a market. Like watching the price history of the stock market, you are unlikely to predict when or where the bottom of this downward movement will be. It's advisable to be very selective in making purchases at this time. You know a bottom is coming, so it may be advantageous to maintain your cash position to increase purchase power for the future. The best deals during this period are going to be deals that generate strong cash flow so that in the event rents decline, you will still be protected. Knowing just how far home values and rent rates will fall is a period of uncertainty.

Phase 4. Demand is increasing due to fewer properties available on the market. Indicators of this phase include:

- Short time on market.
- Decreasing unemployment numbers.
- Uptick in property flips or renovations.
- Slowly increasing home values and rent rates after reaching their lowest points.
- Decreasing bank foreclosure inventory due to competition for these homes.

This is the best time to buy because from here on out, the homes will be increasing in value, and you will be earning equity appreciation and rent increases as the market recovers. You'll want to find a way to buy as much as you can at this time because good deals will become great deals eventually. Be as greedy as you can and find ways to partner or secure other sources of lending because it could be very soon that the values start skyrocketing, and you will have tons of options to sell, refinance, or simply accumulate more cash flow.

Taxes. An often-overlooked item by new and old investors alike is the tax structure. How are property taxes currently assessed in the town? Does the local township levy a tax on rental property owners in addition to property tax? How often do they reassess tax values? Some towns reevaluate every three years, some annually, and some haven't made any adjustments in over ten years.

A personal example is when I purchased a duplex in Columbus, Ohio on the Ohio State University campus. The home was currently assessed at $225,000 and the taxes were $4,500 for the year. My cash flow projections were amazing. After purchasing the home for $320,000, the next year the board of education assessed my property at $320,000 and increased my taxes to $8,600. That decreased my cash flow by $341 a month! Fortunately, due to the low interest rate I had received through my VA Loan and excessive rent rates from being on a college campus, I was still able to meet my minimum cash flow requirements.

Additionally, you can always appeal the tax assessment and oftentimes negotiate lower. I was able to appeal the assessment down to $275,000 using comparable homes in the area and that brought my cash flow up some. Learning from this, I now always contact the county and town tax assessor to learn about their structure and get much more accurate forecasting when conducting my deal analysis.

How to: I go to Google and search "[name of county] county tax lookup" and that typically directs me to an online portal where I can search tax information and history about a property. If unavailable, there should be a phone number of the office listed on the page, and you can reach out to them for more information. Once you find the property, you will be able to identify the value it is currently being assessed at, the rate or amount in dollars of tax being levied, and whether it is classified as residential or commercial. If the only information provided is the millage rate, you can simply do a calculation based on the purchase price of the home multiplied by the millage rate to find what you can expect to pay in tax. (purchase price of the home) x (millage rate) = tax rate or payment

From this point, call the assessor's office to learn about their reevaluation process and the implications it would have on your purchase and then plug in those new numbers into your spreadsheet.

Another thing to consider is the fact that some towns charge a rental license fee, charge a business registration fee, and levy additional taxes on the gross rents earned (Mercantile Tax). For example, a property I recently purchased charges a twenty-five-dollar annual rental license fee, a fifty-dollar onetime business registration fee, and a .0015% Mercantile Tax on gross rents earned from the previous year.

Insurance. You are going to need homeowner's insurance. The coverage and limits you request determine the price of the policy. It would be in your best interest to gather up as much data about your property as you can. This information will help you shop for quotes on home insurance and other unrelated insurances as well—all at once. For example, sometimes—though not always—you may find that if you bundle your home insurance with your auto insurance, you will receive a savings on both.

Data or information to gather about your property: size of the home in square feet, year the home was built, construction materials of the home (wood, brick, etc.), if you have pets (you will have to disclose to the insurance company the type of pet and quantity, for some companies will not insure people with, for example, dangerous breeds), your history of home insurance claims (whether you've filed any claims within the last three to five years), and recent internal or external renovations or upgrades to the home.

Factors that affect the price of your policy based on the house: location, size, age, building materials, renovations and updates, and security systems.

Location: The location of the home increases the cost of the policy if the adjusters believe the home to be in a high-risk area, likewise the premium would be lower in a low-risk area. High-crime areas increase the premium rate. The proximity of the house to a fire station and the quality of the house's fire protection lowers the premium. For example, being within five miles of a fire station lowers the rate as opposed to living in a more rural area serviced by volunteer firefighters.

Homes located in areas prone to tornadoes cost more to insure—such as, Louisiana, Iowa, and Mississippi—as they're located in Tornado Alley. Florida and Texas homes cost more to insure as they are prone to hurricanes. States with the highest average annual homeowner's insurance include Louisiana, Florida, Texas, Oklahoma, and Kansas. Lowest average annual insurance rates include Oregon, Utah, Idaho, Nevada, and Wisconsin.

Most standard policies do not cover floods or earthquakes, so you will need to shop for a company that does include them in their standard policies or purchase additional insurance for that specific need. Most insurance companies also offer discounts for improvements that reduce claims like, for example, impact-resistant roofs that can withstand hailstorms. Ask to see where and how you can save based upon where your house is situated.

Age: Older homes typically cost more to insure than a new construction because oftentimes if a repair is needed, the scope of the job may require more work to bring the 1920s-built home up to the building code of the 2020s. For example, if you need to repair a toilet or renovate a bathroom where the toilet was previously twelve inches from the wall, and the new code dictates that the toilet must be fifteen inches from the wall, you now have to spend the money to blow out and frame a new wall in order to have the required clearance. On average ordinarily, insurers charge raise their rates 1% increase for a 30-year-old home, 2% for a 35-year-old home, and 3% for a 50-year-old home.

Construction: Brick homes cost 6% less to insure on average and homes made of fire-resistive materials save 12%. Newly constructed homes get an average of 36% discount compared to other homes.

Renovations: Renovations such as a metal roof or weatherproof windows will lower your premium because it reduces your likelihood of filing a claim. Renovations—like including a pool or an addition—may increase the value of the home, but also increase the insurance rate.

Security: Security systems and smoke detectors not only protect your house by providing an early warning against danger or disaster but also typically lead to a lower rate and additional discounts.

You, the homeowner: Younger buyers may pay a higher premium than older buyers. as a reflection of The former poses a higher risk because of due to evidence of shorter work history or statistics based on age of people that default on loans is more prone to default on loans according to statistics based on age. Married couples likewise receive lower premiums as they reflect more stability and settlement into a lifestyle. Pets will drive up the cost of the insurance and some breeds of dogs aren't insurable or require separate coverages as an add-on—as mentioned above. Your credit score also can determine your premium such as a higher credit score yields you a lower premium.

Coverages: Typically, you will have the option to insure for the Actual Cash Value (ACV) or the Replacement Cost Value (RCV) coverage. Actual cash will have a lower payout to you in the event your house burns to the ground; however, it also comes with a less expensive policy price. The replacement value will be a more expensive premium than the ACV; however, for many homeowners, it is worth the difference because of the value of the belongings they have in their homes. There are home insurance policies designated Ho1 through Ho8. I'll briefly describe each.

Ho1. This is the homeowner's policy basic form. You are only covered if the damage was caused by something specifically named on the policy—for example, an explosion. Any damage occurring outside of what is specifically named will not be covered under this policy.

Ho2. This is the homeowner's policy broad form. The Ho2 is considered an RCV policy, for it includes more named perils. With this policy, make sure to understand if you as the homeowner pay for the damage and are later reimbursed or if the costs will be covered directly from the insurance provider.

H03. This is your standard homeowner policy. More to follow on this.

H04. This is the homeowner's policy tenant form. The H04 is typically referred to as renter's insurance, it offers coverage for personal property damaged by the perils named in H02.

H05. This is the homeowner's policy comprehensive form. H05 provides the most protection and the highest coverage limits, as well as the highest premium because it covers more. The main difference between H05 and H03 is that the H03 covers all risk to the structure of the home, but the personal property is only covered if it is specifically named in the policy.

The H05 policy covers all risk to the structure of the home as well as everything in the home unless you specifically choose to exclude certain items. For your own awareness, it is important to find out what items are exempted from your policy regardless of whether you select a H03 or H05 policy.

H06. This is the homeowner's policy condominium form. Condo insurance with the same coverage as H02.

H07. Homeowner's policy mobile home form. Same coverage as the H03 but specifically for mobile or manufactured homes.

<u>Ho8</u>. Homeowner's modified form. This is for homes that are over fifty-one years old or are valued at less than $200,000. This policy provides the least amount of coverage. It is essentially a bare-bones coverage in which the burden to recover from damage relies mostly on the homeowner.

In-home business policy. Some insurance providers offer an in-home business policy. This could be added in addition to your Ho policy (listed above) or as its own policy, depending on the provider. In short, if you have a work-from-home business, you can insure the business property for up to $10,000 and receive general liability coverage up to $1 million. If you must close your business because of damage to the home, the policy will also cover income the business loses and ongoing expenses for up to one year.

Bottom Line: The type of insurance and coverage will vary depending on each person and how much they value what is in the home. I would recommend clearly understanding what is outlined in the policies and comparing the same coverages with multiple providers for the best rate. It may be that you will find insurance for very cheap, however, the language used in the policy may provide enough wiggle room for the insurance companies to not fully pay out for damages. It is worth the extra couple bucks to know how the insurance company will pay out and take care of you given any scenario.

Local Laws. It's in your best interest to identify whether the state you're operating in is more tenant or landlord friendly when it comes to laws and regulations. Again, you can google the city's rental regulations and browse through their codes or laws to know what to expect from them in operating your rental. This information is necessary because it will dictate how you structure your leases to best protect yourself. For example, it may be a tenant-friendly state and have an in-depth process when it comes to evictions. Knowing the eviction process will help you clearly identify your lease terms and help you decide if it would be better to put tenants on a month-to-month or yearlong lease.

Other things such as noncompliance and ordinance fees will be explained in the code, and you would be wise to include that in your lease. For instance, things as detailed as how high the grass can be before the town charges you a fee for noncompliance. The more specifics you have in your lease, the easier it will be to justify your case if you find yourself in a situation where you end up in court to evict a tenant.

Rent Rates. One of the most important subjects to be knowledgeable about is the rent rates in your market. You need to be able to identify what the range is and know that it will vary by the street, amenities offered, parking options, pet tolerance, lawn size, property class, and the number of bedrooms and bathrooms. Wisdom is achieved in counsel and your best bet is to utilize all the resources available to you to form your own knowledge. I'll list some methods I use below.

Basic Allowance for Housing (BAH) rating. One of the easiest methods for determining your rent rate would be to start with your duty station's BAH rate or even the BAH rate for your zip code if you're not on active duty. BAH rates are evaluated yearly by considering the median market rent, average utilities, and average renter's insurance. Therefore, the amounts typically fluctuate every year. The intent of BAH is to cover approximately 90% of the service member's housing cost. It's broken down into six standard housing profiles derived from the Department of Defense Travel Management Office BAH Policy.

Profile	Grade with Dependents	Grade without Dependents
1 Bedroom Apartment		E-1, E-2, E-3, E-4
2 Bedroom Apartment		O-1
2 Bedroom Townhouse	E-5	O-1E
3 Bedroom Townhouse	E-6	O-3E
3 Bedroom House	W-3	O-6

Knowing this, you're able to visualize what rank of tenant your property would attract and market it accordingly for the shortest amount of vacancy time. Is it a 3-bedroom house near the base, but not the highest property class? Suppose that a single E-5 BAH is $1,050 a month. You have multiple options. You could market towards a single E-5 near that price point and hope for a longer-term tenant.

Another option would be to market for a lower enlisted (E1-E4) with dependents for a little bit of a premium. A final option would be to market the property for three E-5 and below tenants at $1,200 a month. The latter are still getting a good deal at $400 a month per person in rent, not living on post, and you're receiving a premium over the BAH rating. Know that with this option, you'll likely have a higher turnover and potentially more tenant issues to resolve, but that's also why you're receiving a higher rent rate.

Reverse searching. Use craigslist, Zillow, or Facebook Marketplace as if you were shopping for a place to rent. See what places are going for and what they're offering with that price. A 2-bedroom, 1-bathroom on the same street could vary as much as $300 based on the range of factors outlined in this chapter.

Realtors and property management companies. Additionally, I like to call local management companies and realtors to add more depth to my knowledge of the market. Moreover, these are great connections to have as you scale your business and consulting them on the rates in your market can help build those relationships down the road. They will be able to answer more precisely what factors will help you earn the highest rates in your market.

Department of Housing and Urban Development (HUD) rating. Another useful tool, though sometimes more difficult to track down, is the rate which government assistance deems fair for housing. Some counties list these numbers online, others you must call. For example, the HUD websites that do have the information will tell you the fair market rates for: efficiency apartments, 1-bedroom, 2-bedroom, 3-bedroom, and 4-bedroom homes.

The Office of Policy Development and Research (OPDR), an office within HUD, is a great starting point for finding the fair market rents and keeps a record of a few years back that you can cross-reference with. A note on this, your results will vary depending on the township your properties are located in. The housing director in the township of my first HUD-assisted rental felt it was her duty to negotiate on behalf of the tenant and did not permit me to charge the max rate on the HUD website.

This can be overcome through time and building a better relationship with the office. Another strategy can be to improve the property, and when you go for your yearly inspections and lease renewal, you can plead your case as to why the improvements or conditions have justified the rent increase.

Now with all this gleaned information, you should very easily be able to determine the rent rate you may charge for the home you're purchasing. When working through your spreadsheets, it's always good to make three models:

- Model 1: Property as-is
- Model 2: Moderate rent increase
- Model 3: Performance at the max rate

Let's say you are purchasing a triplex as an owner occupant that is currently renting for $1,000 per unit.

In Model 1, you can show a gross monthly rent of $2,000. This is reflective of how the property will perform the day you buy it. In Model 2, you can show how all three units will be producing $1,000 per unit in gross rent or you can show that you are still living there and increased the rent a moderate amount $1,050 per unit. For Model 3, you can show three units rented at top-of-market rates, maybe renting at $1,200 per unit for a total of $3,600 in gross rents. Additionally, there are other ways you can monetize the property such as rent for the garage, parking spaces, Airbnb, etc.

Environmental Factors. Take into consideration the environmental factors that can affect the purchase of your home—such as, location, air and water quality, soil conditions, wetlands, and climate.

Location, location, location is probably the most associated phrase people think of when they think of "real estate." This is true for a myriad of reasons, but especially for development and homeownership—and of course for rentals. First, people are always going to need a place to live and there will never be enough financial readiness for every single person in this country to buy a home, so rentals will never go away. With that being said, a home built on a busy road, underneath power lines, and next to a large chemical plant will never attract as high of a rent as a home tucked away on a quiet road or a home situated within the confines of a city with many retail and transportation options.

Think; for example, what is your property located near to that would be a detriment to the lifestyle quality of the people living there? Especially in the beginning of your real estate investing career, it is important to physically drive to and around the property to get an intimate knowledge of the area. The house may look great from the pictures, but a hundred yards behind it is one of the most foul-smelling water treatment plants that you would have only noticed from driving around. If driving around the property isn't an option for you, using Google Earth to get a bird's-eye view of the surrounding area may suffice for identifying manufacturing facilities, heavily semitruck-trafficked roads, power lines, windmills, trailer parks, etc. Unless you are getting the home at an unbelievably low price, you're better off steering clear of these types of properties.

Air, water, and soil conditions. I did my first "fix and flip" home in New Jersey. At that time, I had the knowledge—through seeking counseling from more experienced buyers and professionals in the field—that houses without a septic system would not be eligible for a loan with most lenders. It either had to have one already or have one installed within sixty days of closing. We looked through the property, conducted our own inspection, and even held evidence that in the seller's disclosure it listed that there was a septic system on the property. Great. Fast-forward six months—when it came time to sell and we wanted to verify the exact location of the septic tank—we were dejected with the news that the property did not in fact have a septic system, and the price tag for installing one would be $30,000.

There are pros and cons to waiving your inspection rights when purchasing an investment property. One of the biggest cons to waiving your inspection right is that you also waive your right to sue the seller down the road if there is any fraudulence in the disclosure of the home. This took a "home run" deal down to a "base hit," but the learning experience along the way was worth it.

When we flipped the home, we ended up negotiating a lower sale price with the buyer and were still able to quickly sell it. With what I know now, I always confirm the type of sewage the home is using. If it's city sewage, great. If not, I confirm if the home is using a cesspool or septic system, and I include language in the purchase agreement to protect myself. This way, I have the ability to back out of the deal or use that information for leverage, depending on the setup. A lot of states aren't as bothersome as New Jersey in this regard, but it is a costly "line item" that could alter the success of your deal if not discovered.

Air quality. As far as air quality is concerned, once again location plays a large role in this effect. In many western states, smog and wildfire haze can be a contributing factor to the desirability of certain homes. Wildfires are unpredictable and are dealt with as they evidence themselves. However, if the home is in an area that is likely to experience wildfire smoke or is even in the path to a wildfire, it may be a deal breaker—especially depending on the insurance quotes given for your cash flow estimates.

Water quality. In most purchases, the lender will require a water test to determine the potability of the water. However, even if the results come back that the water is acidic—meaning it shows a low pH—banks will still lend. The consideration, though, is if the home is older and has been running acidic water through the pipes for many years. Although the lender may still approve the loan, this will inevitably deteriorate the pipes and lead to extensive plumbing repairs. A negotiating piece for purchasing a home with low pH would be for the seller to concede cash to purchase a water-treatment setup, or to set one up themselves prior to closing. Depending on your situation (whether you may require a water softener, acid neutralizer, or sulfuric water treatment), costs can vary from $1,000 to $7,500. Along with a low pH deteriorating your pipes, it's also not the best for your health if you consume most of your water from the tap.

Soil conditions. Oftentimes, areas will be known for likelihood of sinkholes. Florida, Texas, Alabama, Missouri, Kentucky, Tennessee, and Pennsylvania are states that are known to have areas prone to sinkholes. A sinkhole will evidence itself in a region where the soluble types of rocks below the land surface can naturally be dissolved by the water circulating through them. Rocks like salt beds, domes, gypsum, limestone, and other carbonate rocks are known as soluble. Walking the property will readily show evidence of sinkholes by round circular or localized depressions in the property land or foundation settling. Foundational issues are very costly repairs so going through the basement and looking for uneven floors, cracks in the floor or walls, cabinets leaning from the wall, or doors and windows that won't open will be an indicator of potential foundational or settling issues.

Wetlands. Wetlands are areas that are saturated with water either seasonally or permanently like swamps, marshes, creeks, rivers, ponds, and bogs. They have a specific ecosystem of plants and animals and aid in flood control and water quality. You can check with US Fish & Wildlife Services in your area to see if the property in consideration falls under wetlands classification. The significance of wetlands classification is the challenge to develop on a property in close proximity to wetlands.

You will need to contact the Army Corps of Engineers or the Environmental Protection Agency (EPA) to request a permit to build. They will review your request and may give you a no permit required or inform you of the restrictions in development. Note that it is illegal to begin construction without a permit in this type of situation, so be sure to confirm your plans before executing.

Most often, wetlands decrease the value of the property because you may be unable to further develop what is already pre-existing. Each situation will be different, and the EPA will be able to provide guidance as to what is possible with your specific situation. I once almost closed on a land purchase that had wetlands classification, but fortunately I learned about the permit requirements. As it turned out, after the request review, I was informed I would be unable to build a home on this land. That property remained vacant for quite a few years and dropped significantly in value because of this. On the other hand, wetlands that are amenities like ponds or lakes, add value to the property because homeowners find those amenities to be desirable.

Climate. Depending on the geographic location, certain markets may be prone to specific climate hazards such as flooding, hurricane, hail, tornado, blizzard, thunderstorm, and extreme temperatures. While it is hard to determine how much those factors effect home values, it is known that those climate risks will increase insurance premiums because of the risk they carry. So, if you are researching a new market to invest in, be sure to do some research on any common climate hazards or reach out to insurance companies for more information on that specific area.

Socioeconomic Factors. Socioeconomic factors include people's occupation, education, income, wealth, and place of residence. To keep things simple, we'll break them down into two subsets: higher socioeconomic regions and lower socioeconomic regions.

Lower Socioeconomic Regions: People in lower socioeconomic areas pay higher than average rents relative to house prices in the area. This is because ownership costs for landlords in these areas are higher than those of higher socioeconomic regions.

Landlords are justified in charging a premium due to certain tendencies in these areas—such as, higher turnover rates, higher rates of rental default or arrears, or higher rates of property damage. More rural, blue-collar areas where tenants typically rent for longer periods of time and respect the property as if it were their own, pose less of a financial risk to the landlord in terms of rent default or property damage.

Neighborhoods that have higher crime rates and foreclosures typically rent at a lower cost.

Higher Socioeconomic Regions: People in higher socioeconomic areas pay average or even lower rents relative to house prices in the area. There is a lower risk premium applied to higher socioeconomic regions because typically there are lower rates of rental default, property damage, or turnover.

Additionally, since renting high-valued homes typically will not earn the landlord large profit margins comparatively to low-valued homes, the rent rate will land much closer to the landlord's monthly mortgage payment.

*Note, however, that rent rates will match people's ability to pay them, regardless of the region.

Rent-to-Income (RTI) Ratios. Your biggest concern as a landlord is in your tenant's ability to pay their rent each month. Evictions, on average, cost $3,500—so it pays to screen your tenants accurately. The RTI ratio determines the monthly gross income a tenant should earn to be able to afford rent each month—the standard is 30%. You can easily do this math by multiplying their gross monthly income by .3 to get their monthly rental income.

$$(\$4,000) \times (.3) = (\$1,200).$$

This is most applicable in areas with a lower salary average as those demographics typically spend a greater percentage of their income on rent. In many markets, however, renters are high earners, and someone making $300,000 a year is most likely not renting a place for $7,500 a month. Knowing this will help you in identifying if a prospective tenant will likely pay their rent but will also enable you to search for market demographics and find one that aligns with your niche.

It is important to become knowledgeable about the socioeconomic factors involved in your market to build a better strategy in choosing the location of your properties. Much of this information can be ascertained through your local government website or library, the United States Census Bureau website, or the Urban Institute website. This information will not only educate you on the best areas to invest but will also give you a better understanding of these options.

If you're looking into a prominent college town for example, you have the option of renting to students, young professionals, hospital or university employees, as well as the option to rent as an Airbnb or corporate housing. On the other hand, if you are looking into a more rural area, you may find that your options of prospective renters are much more limited, and it may lead to longer periods of vacancies in between tenants. Now, there are pros and cons to both. If you're renting to university students, you will be able to charge higher premiums but are faced with turnover and potential damage each year. More suburban or rural areas typically lead to much longer tenant occupation.

Permanent Change of Station (PCS) or PCS'ing. All the research you've conducted up to this point is great. You've set your goals, made your plan of action, and are actively seeking to get deals done. Don't slap that BUY button just yet. One important consideration in your due diligence is the likelihood of when and where your next PCS will be. Do you have goals within the military that will cause you to attend a selection and relocate? What if you get injured or dropped from the course, where will they send you? Does your career path funnel service members to certain locations as they promote?

How many more years do you intend to serve and where do you want to live afterward? This type of forward-looking perspective is crucial in determining the viability of creating your rental empire. Getting the real estate investing "bug" and rushing off to land your first deal is exciting, but how much of a mess will you be in if three months after owning the property, you get stationed in Germany? For this reason, I would venture to say that it would be a good idea to factor in property management into your deal analysis.

Now, if the property is only profitable without management and you have to relocate and hire a property management company, then you may end up paying for something each month that was intended to pay you instead.

Property Management. Each person's situation will be different and their tolerance for stress and multitasking as well, so there is no rule of thumb for exactly how many units you can handle before hiring a property manager. In many cases, as long as you have built up a team of people to repair the property when situations arise, show and fill the property with tenants, and have a way to communicate while deployed or in long-distance, you may never need a management company.

In your due diligence, it would be prudent to account for the use of a property manager. I suggest this for two reasons. One, you'll want to identify whom you would work with before actually needing them so that—in the event a last-minute situation arises— you'll confidently be able to select a competent company when needed. Second, you'll know beforehand the impact of their cost on your cash flow in the near and far term. For example, you may not utilize a property manager for your first few years— thus allowing you to save more money to fund future deals—and wait to do so when you've reached a portfolio size where the cost isn't a significant disruption to your cash flow. Now, when you do hire one, you are more informed as to how your properties will be performing with this added expense.

Depends on the market, but typically property managers will charge a monthly fee of 8–10% of gross rents and either a full or half month's rent as a leasing fee. Each company is different, and some may charge less per door (based on the number of units), but more for leasing and service fees. It's important to vet the company you intend to work with, and you must train them in how you want the property to be operated and how you will communicate with each other. On the flip side, if your property is profitable after factoring in a property management fee and there isn't an immediate need to use them, then you've found a great deal and will enjoy some nice cash flow.

Later in Chapter 7, I will go further into the details of one of my property management experiences and explain systems I have used to eliminate the need for one. With the digital age we now live in, almost anything can be accomplished over the phone or through an app. I have lists of repairmen for each category: Heating, Ventilation, and Air Conditioning (HVAC); plumbing, electrical, carpentry, and a general handyman. My tenants pay electronically, and I use a rental property management app as a medium to communicate with them. So now when I'm overseas, I am able to see their maintenance requests, track lease expirations, and collect rent—all through Wi-Fi.

I contact my tenants, contractors, and local realtors before a deployment and give them a heads-up that I will be emailing or communicating with them through WhatsApp. Depending on operational tempo, I am usually able to respond to situations in less than two days and have emergency criteria in place. Before I leave, I email each tenant a list of contacts for repairs. I let them know that only in an emergency (e.g., a pipe that burst), they should call down the line of the provided list until someone can come and repair it. Those contractors know they can bill me electronically, or I can mail a check that will arrive within two weeks.

The more experienced you get, the more systems you should be creating to further automate and scale your business.

Finding good deals. If you can, picture yourself on a tropical paradise for a second. Imagine that everyone on your cruise ship disembarked and were allowed two days of exploration on the island. Well, those two days have come and gone, and you've found upon your return that the boat has sunk. There's no food left. Everyone has to fend for themself with what is available on the island. Naturally, everyone is going to begin searching for food and grab whatever is most readily available to them. They'll come across an apple tree and grab the apples they can reach.

The low-hanging fruits. Without exception, most everyone can reach the same heights and the availability of good, ripe fruit is becoming scarce. You're able to take a step back and look objectively at what is going on in the "market." The supply is dwindling, yet the demand is remaining equal. This is increasing the value of the fruits. In order to sidestep this fierce competition or pay exorbitant prices for the fruits, you look inward for intuition and strategy to find a way to maintain your supply of fruits uninterrupted. Alas, you decide to build a ladder out of tree branches and climb to the top of trees—where everyone else has been unable to reach—and secure delicious, ripe fruits for your own sustenance.

This is a silly example, but it demonstrates quite a few things. First, the "law of supply and demand." You'll notice that there are only so many fruit trees, yet there is a continuous demand for the fruit. Economics 101, this increases the value of the fruit much like the prices of homes in a buyer's market.

Second, notice how everyone initially goes for the low-hanging fruit. People, like woodland animals, instinctively go for the path of least resistance. Many will be unable to break from the mold of looking for this low-hanging fruit and will complain that they aren't getting enough or have to pay too much—when all they had to do was change their perspective, take decisive action, and get the fruit themselves.

That's where you come in. You're not going to be doing what everybody else is doing. You won't be putting up with the shenanigans of competing for the same fruits when you can creatively come up with a means to access your own supply. You come up with the conduit—building a ladder—that equates to networking, researching, and finding off-market deals to gather your fruits or, in this case, rental properties.

Too often, aspiring real estate investors take the mainstream approach of working with a realtor to find an investment property that becomes available on the Multiple Listing Service (MLS). While undoubtedly there are deals to be found on the MLS, there is untapped potential for off-market deals as well. As the population in the United States increases, people are moving away from major metropolitan areas to more rural and affordable locations—especially in the work-from-home era. The raw land and previously installed infrastructure become more valuable as they are finite resources.

You'll notice the MLS hosts the most competition for good deals because that's where the majority of people are looking. In this case, you're likely to enter a "highest and best offer" scenario which may exceed your purchase criteria and lose the deal.

I will describe below the most all-encompassing means I am aware of for finding deals, so you can read through and put these tools in your toolbox to hopefully implement with great success.

Looking on the Multi Listing Service (MLS). This goes without saying but have a realtor add you to their email chain lists, specifically the ones that fit your specific criteria. On a daily basis, you should be getting emails and there should be enough information provided for you to run it through your analysis software and determine if you need to act on the property or not.

Drive around your target market. Pull up Google Maps, identify the region you're looking to invest in. Label corridors to segment the region into manageable routes. Spend time driving through those segments looking for properties that have "for sale by owner" signs, look unkempt, or just look like they're being used as a rental. Write the addresses down, check with the county tax office to see who owns it, and try to find a way to give that person a call or mail them a letter. You'd be surprised at how many landlords are burnt-out from the business and would be eager to take you up on an offer to sell.

Expand your network. Start getting involved in more community-driven organizations, clubs, or churches. As you meet people and establish more relationships in the area, don't shy away from letting them know what you're into and what you're looking for. People can't help you if they don't know, and most people are glad to share a connection or steer you in the right direction. It's human nature to help others, just don't come across as a transactional type of person. Genuinely build rapport, it will take you much further.

Find real estate investing clubs. You can google "real estate investing clubs near me" and come up with a multitude of options. Meetup, for example, is a website that many real estate clubs use to post their meetings on. If you don't find one to your liking, create your own! Nowadays with how digital everything has become, you can join networks across the country, but just know you'll be best served for deals by working with people in your area. There is a lot of knowledge to be gained from joining other groups—but try to begin within your area first.

Identify properties based on record searches. You can call the county courthouse or browse online, but there are lists available which show:

- Properties that are in pre-foreclosure.
- Eviction records. You can look up the address and maybe find a burnt-out landlord willing to make a deal.
- Inheritance or estate sales.
- Divorce settlements.
- Tax liens.

This list qualifies sellers as motivated, and you may find that some of your best deals can come from these situations.

Online Market Places. Explore online through craigslist, Facebook Marketplace, ForSaleByOwner,

Zillow, Trulia, and Realtor.com. Browse your local-services platform and local newspapers online. Look for the "for sale" ads but also post your own ad of what you're looking for.

Email lists. Get in touch with wholesalers and larger investment companies in the area, let them know what you're looking for, and ask to be included in their mailing lists (to receive notifications when properties become available). Just because someone is wholesaling the property doesn't mean it's not a good deal. When done correctly, the wholesaler can be compensated and allow you a profitable opportunity for a win-win scenario.

You never know what "simply asking the question or making the phone call" will get you, so take the action. On one occasion, I purchased a home within a row of homes and met the neighbor my first day working on the property. The neighbor was happy to see me working to rehab the property and take care of it, complaining that her landlord never took care of her issues and that she was looking to move out. I contacted her landlord and was able to strike a deal with them in two phone calls. Never would have happened had I not decided to take the chance, just to see "what if." So, I encourage you to embody the same mindset, put it out there—and often.

Check on Learning:

1. What are the topics to consider when conducting Due Diligence?

- Mindset

- Market Phases

- Taxes

- Insurance

- Local Laws

- Rent Rates

- Environmental Factors

- Socioeconomic Factors

- Permanent Change of Station (PCS) likelihood

- Property Management

2. Where can you find good deals?

- MLS

- Driving around within your market

- Your Network

- Real Estate Investing Clubs

- Record Searches

- Online Market Places: Craigslist, Facebook Marketplace, Zillow, Trulia, Realtor.com, etc.

- Wholesalers and Email Lists

Chapter 6

THE DEAL

Deal Analysis. At this point you've completed your market research and due diligence, so it is time to put the abstract into numbers. *You will need the following information about your deal:*

Purchase Price	Annual Insurance	Rent Rate(s)
Length of Loan	Annual Tax	Market Valuation
Loan Interest Rate	Utilities Estimate	Comparables

Using this data, it will be a very quick "plug and play" with this simple deal analyzer using Microsoft Excel or Google Sheets. There are many variations of this online and there's even some fancy software that have built-in calculators, nice cover sheets, and pdf generators. I like to keep it simple. I created my own spreadsheet which is available to download for free online at to www.thecashflowcommando.com.

Property Address	City, State	County	Zip	Type	Where Found	Link			
123 Example St	City, CT	Green	12345	Triplex	Zillow	www.zillow.com/house			
Costs & Values	**$**	**Units**	**Rents ($)**	**Expenses**	**$**	**% of Rent**	**Totals**	**Monthly**	**Yearly**
Purchase Price	$419,580	406 Aaron St	Owner Occupy	Mortgage	$1,706.77		Income	$2,600	$31,200
Closing Costs	$8,392	408 Aaron St		Taxes	$325.00		Expenses	$2,400	$28,801
Estimated Repairs	$0	410 Aaron St		Insurance	$108.33		Cash Flow	$200	$2,399
Total Project Cost	$427,972	Unit 4		Water / Sewer	$0.00		Cap Rate	6.20%	
After Repair Value		Unit 5		Trash	$0.00		Cash on Cash RoI	160%	
		Unit 6		Electric	$0.00		Gross Rent Multiplier	13.45	
Cash to Close	$1,500	Unit 7		Natural Gas	$0.00		Cash Needed	$9,892	
Loan Amount	$418,080	Unit 8		HOA	$0.00		Yrs to recover	4.12	
Amortization	30	Unit 9		Lawn/Snow	$0.00	0%	Price per unit	$139,860	
Interest Rate	2.75%	Unit 10		Vacancy	$130.00	5%			
Insurance	$1,300	Unit 11		Repairs	$130.00	5%			
Tax	$3,900	Unit 12		CapEx	$0.00	0%			
	Total	Total	$2,600	Total	$2,400.11				

Instructions:

1. In Row #2, fill out the property address, the style of home, and where you found it—so you can easily reference it at a later point.

2. In Column B, insert all of your collected information into the respective yellow cells. This will auto populate fields in column F.

3. In Column D, insert the rent rate you will expect to receive.

Note: You can slice this however you like. If you are house hacking with some roommates, list the amount of rent you will be charging them to see how it helps offset your monthly mortgage payments. If you are living in a multifamily unit, look at the numbers both with one unit vacant (the one you will be living in) as well as with all units rented out to show how the property will perform once you move out.

4. In Column G, simply allocate percentages to the respective operating costs. I typically allocate a total of 10% of the gross rent to things such as repairs, vacancies, and capital expenditures. If you intend to outsource lawn care or snowplowing (if the property even needs it), then enter in an estimate that would be spread out over the course of one year.

5. Once all required fields have been filled with data, check out columns I & J.

How to best use this tool:

Software and Applications: I designed this simple calculator to enable me to analyze thousands of deals more quickly and efficiently. First, I would find a property from the Multi Listing Service (MLS), craigslist, Zillow, or even from driving around. Next, I would open my template in Google Sheets, duplicate this worksheet, and begin entering in the information about the property in consideration. It was very convenient to use Google Sheets from my iPhone while out and about or on-site even, as it works that quickly and enables me to make more informed and quicker decisions.

How to use Column H:

Cash Flow: Cash flow is what you can expect to put into your pocket each month. When considering a property to put under contract, you must ensure it aligns with your specific niche or criteria. If you are solely investing for cash flow, you should have a predetermined baseline amount and not stray significantly away from it unless you have a value-added justification. For example, if your goal is to have

$450 per month in net cash flow and the home only produces $350, it isn't necessarily a deal breaker.

Pro Tip: It isn't necessarily a deal breaker! Making great real estate purchases involve looking at a deal in multiple layers as well as in multiple years and forecasting possibilities. It is not as cut-and-dried as, "if my cash flow number isn't met, it's not a good deal." You will miss a lot of opportunities if you utilize this binary approach.

There may be potential opportunities; for example, the home isn't currently renting for market rates, but once you increase the rent you will meet your target. Another good scenario could be if you are able to purchase the home with close to or more than 20% equity in it the day you close. This will enable you to refinance into a conventional loan without paying the Private Mortgage Insurance (PMI) and recycle your VA Loan quicker. If you're able to add some more value to the home, you could utilize a home-equity line of credit or refinance and have access to more money to use for future investments. It's half art, half science, but it totally requires multilayered thinking of how to monetize the property. This is also your competitive advantage, being able to see future potential in a home that the competition can't see—so you are able to structure a better offer to make the deal work.

On the flip side, do not get emotionally attached to the house either and try to fudge the numbers so that it meets your criteria. Always err on the side of caution, and if anything, increase the percentage amount you have allocated towards vacancies, repairs, and capital expenditure (or capex). This is to make sure you're giving it an unbiased look and making sure the deal still works for you under what may be worst-case scenarios. It is a very defeating feeling to have a number in mind that you expect to earn only to realize you were looking through rose-colored glasses, and— as each month passes—you don't hit that number.

Capitalization Rate (Cap Rate): The cap rate is the rate of return yielded from the property by comparing the income the property produces to the value of the property, assuming no loan was used to purchase it. It's most useful as a tool to compare the value of similar deals. So, imagine you purchase a property for $500,000 cash which has a stabilized Net Operating Income (NOI) of $25,000. This would mean you have a 5% cap rate. Knowing that, anytime you look at a property for sale which includes the cap rate percentage, you can quickly estimate the NOI in your head with some simple math. If I see a property listed for sale at $500,000 with a 5% cap rate, I know I will most likely not take the deal if I am financing it through a bank because after mortgage payments, there would not be enough cash flow in the deal for my

preferences.
It is calculated by dividing the NOI by the property's value and expressed as a percentage.

In our spreadsheet example, the NOI is calculated by the   following:

Total Annualized Rents ($2,600) x (12) =
$31,200
Minus Operating Expenses, excluding mortgage
($433.33) x (12) = $5,199.96 (31,200) – (5,199.96) =
26,000
NOI = 26,000
Divided by Home Value ($419,580)
(26,000) / (419,580) = 0.0619

Multiplied by 100 to get a percentage.
(0.0619) x (100) = 6.196

Total Rents	$2,600.00
Less	
Taxes	$325.00
Insurance	$108.33
Water / Sewer	$0.00
Trash	$0.00
Electric	$0.00
Natural Gas	$0.00
	6.20%

In this property example, the **Cap Rate is 6.2%.** Cap rates can also be used to generate the value of a property if a specific market has an average cap rate. For example, dividing your NOI by the cap rate will give you the value of the home. From our spreadsheet example, it would look like this:

($26,000) / (6.2%) = $419,355 Value of Home

Likewise, the cap rate can be used to roughly estimate the net operating income (NOI) of a home.

($419,580) x (6.2%) = $26,013 Net Operating Income (NOI)

Keep in mind, there are limitations with utilizing the cap rate. Your most accurate number will be using the current market value of the home as opposed to the purchase price. This is because you could either be getting a great deal or overpaying for the home, so using the purchase price cap rate wouldn't enable you to objectively look at the property.

Cap rate can also be utilized in estimating investment risk. A higher cap rate typically dictates a higher level of risk. Inversely, the lower the cap rate, the higher the return on investment and lower level of risk. Think about investing into a 10-year US Treasury bond offering a 3% yield annually. Bonds are possibly the safest investment vehicle and that is why they have such low yield percentages. Consider the bond risk-free. Any amount the cap rate is greater than the risk-free rate is called the risk premium. The risk premium reflects all the additional risks you assume over and above the bond such as: age of the property, credit of the tenants, the economic factors of the market, and more. With this understanding, you can decide if the cap rate is high enough to be worth the risk above what is guaranteed by bonds.

They can also be used for trending. If you can find the cap-rate trends over the past few years in a particular sub-market, then you will have an indication of whether that market is heating up with higher property values identified by shrinking cap rates or cooling off due to higher cap rates.

This is another formula that must be considered as part of your multilayered deal analysis. Cap rate cannot be used as a cut-and-dried, go or no-go criteria. It is best served as a tool to validate the valuation of the property based on your market averages. Cap rate accounts for income and expenses, it can reflect the supply and demand of a market, and is standard verbiage used by investors, lenders, and brokers.

Cash-on-Cash Return on Investment (ROI): Your cash-on-cash return on investment (ROI) is simply the annualized net cash flow divided by the amount you came up with out of pocket to purchase the home. Using the same example from our spreadsheet at the beginning of this chapter, because of the way you can wrap fees into the VA Loan, we only had to come up with $1,500 out of pocket. The property nets you

$2,399 a year. Take that number and divide it by your down payment amount of $1,500. Multiply that by 100 and you get 160%. Show me one stock that guarantees that return in the stock market, I'll wait!

This is the power of the VA Loan. Below is an example of the same property, but with a 20% down payment.

Property Address	City, State	County	Zip	Type	Where Found	Link
123 Example St	City, CT	Green	12345	Triplex	Zillow	www.zillow.com/house

Costs & Values	$	Units	Rents ($)	Expenses	$	% of Rent	Totals	Monthly	Yearly
Purchase Price	$419,580	406 Aaron St	Owner Occupy	Mortgage	$1,370.32		Income	$2,600	$31,200
Closing Costs	$8,392	408 Aaron St	$1,300	Taxes	$325.00		Expenses	$2,064	$24,764
Estimated Repairs	$0	410 Aaron St	$1,300	Insurance	$106.33		Cash Flow	$536	$6,436
Total Project Cost	$427,972	Unit 4		Water / Sewer	$0.00		Cap Rate	6.20%	
After Repair Value		Unit 5		Trash	$0.00		Cash on Cash RoI	8%	
		Unit 6		Electric	$0.00		Gross Rent Multiplier	13.45	
Cash to Close (20%)	$83,916	Unit 7		Natural Gas	$0.00		Cash Needed	$92,308	
Loan Amount	$335,664	Unit 8		HOA	$0.00		Yrs to recover	14.34	
Amortization	30	Unit 9		Lawn/Snow	$0.00	0%	Price per unit	$139,860	
Interest Rate	2.75%	Unit 10		Vacancy	$130.00	5%			
Insurance	$1,300	Unit 11		Repairs	$130.00	5%			
Tax	$3,900	Unit 12		CapEx	$0.00	0%			
		Total		Total	$2,600 Total	$2,063.65			

Here you can see that you now need to come up with $83,916 instead of $1,500, and your monthly cash flow only increased by $336. This took your 160% return on investment (ROI) down to an 8%, which is the industry standard for stock market investing. While $6,436 a year in income sounds much better than $2,399, you only had to spend $1,500 (or one month's BAH payment) to afford this home in the first example. How many years would you have to wait to save up $84,000 and make the same purchase?

When you understand how effective the VA Loan is as a springboard for real estate investing, you are suddenly awakened to an entirely new realm of possibilities on how to escape the rat race. This scenario will be played out more later in the book to show how this single $1,500 investment can, in this manner, lead to more than replacing your military pay within a few years.

Gross Rent Multiplier (GRM): The GRM is the price of the home divided by the rent. In our example:

$$(\$419,580) / (31,200) = 13.45$$

Like cap rate, the GRM is a market-specific number that is best used to validate the valuation of similar deals. It takes much less into consideration and, therefore, shouldn't be used to make a standalone go or no-go decision, however you can simply calculate it on the back of a napkin. The GRM does not account for expenses (whether it is a single-family home or a multifamily home), market factors like supply and demand, or if there are large capital expenditures (capex) expected down the road. It is still good to know as it is also verbiage used by lenders, investors, and brokers. For example, if you know that the GRM in your market is 10, you will look at the gross rents of the property and multiply them by 10 to see if your property is valued within a reasonable range of deviation. The lower the GRM is, the more potentially profitable the deal could be. Continuing on with the example of market GRM of 10, if you notice that the GRM of a property is 11.5, it may be an indicator that you will need to raise rents to market rates.

Otherwise, if you are researching a new market, you can analyze homes currently renting in the area by identifying their gross rent and finding comparable homes or sales history to see what the property is worth. Next, calculate the GRM from those numbers. Now, repeat this process multiple times to get an average GRM for the market.

For example:
- Identify the home composition (number of bedrooms, bathrooms, square footage, amenities).
- Find the listed sale price or purchase price (within 6 months).
- Search through Zillow or other sites to find what that property was charging for rent.

- (Monthly rent) x (12 months) = Annual gross rent
- Sale price of home / Annual gross rent = GRM
- (Property 1 GRM + Property 2 GRM + Property 3 GRM) / # of Properties = Average Market GRM

Cash Needed: The term "cash needed" is self-explanatory. On our spreadsheet, it is the combined amount of closing costs and down payment. This number isn't necessarily the amount you will need to provide as cash out of pocket, since the VA Loan allows you to wrap many of the fees associated with closing into your mortgage. Unfortunately, your lender won't be able to tell you the exact out-of-pocket amount until near the closing date, but they can still give you an accurate estimate very early on.

Years to Recover: I use this metric for my cash utilization strategy. It is simply calculated by taking the amount I had to come up with out of pocket and dividing it by the yearly cash flow I will earn. This is important to keep in mind as you are planning your investment strategy and timeline. You need to be able to understand the following: where your money is going, how much it is earning you, when you will recoup your investment, and how you can best snowball your cash accumulation. With this example, you know that in year 4 (all things remaining equal), you will have recouped your initial investment and will be ready to redeploy it into another investment.

Price per Unit. This is another comparison metric just for situational awareness within your market. Many times, in larger multifamily deals or apartments, there are benchmark averages for price per dwelling unit. Referencing what the spreadsheet informs you about your "price per unit" may enable you to push for more negotiation based on how far-off the average "price per unit" the deal is. For example, if you are buying a 10-unit apartment and the price per unit is $90,000 but the average price per unit in your market for a similar asset is $75,000, you may wish to further analyze ways to get the property for cheaper or generate more income from the property to make it a better deal.

There are a few things to consider when looking at this, however. First, this example assumed that you were paying $1,500 cash to close in addition to $8,392 in closing costs out of pocket. That may not necessarily be the case, depending on how you and your lender structure your deal. If you can wrap that $8,392 into the loan and only need to come up with $1,500, you will earn your money back in half a year!

Also, you must consider the deal with the same scrutiny you would in a chess game. Identify what this purchase would look like in your life: take the additional money you will be able to save from your day job and schedule it to determine how much you will be able to invest by specific dates. For example, by purchasing this home, you will now be able to save all the BAH you receive as well as put another $200 into your pocket. If you're an E5 stationed at Fort Bragg, North Carolina earning $1,410 a month in BAH, you'll now be able to save $1,610 a month or an extra $19,320 a year! Hold that thought, don't go running to the dealership to buy that brand new Camaro at 32% interest with a free tank of gas just yet.

If you remain diligent and work your plan, you will move out of this home after one year to purchase another home. Once you're moved out and the home is completely occupied with tenants, your spreadsheet will now look like this:

Property Address	City, State	County	Zip	Type	Where Found	Link
123 Example St	City, CT	Green	12345	Triplex	Zillow	www.zillow.com/house

Costs & Values	$	Units	Rents ($)	Expenses	$	% of Rent	Totals	Monthly	Yearly
Purchase Price	$419,580	406 Aaron St	$1,300	Mortgage	$1,706.77		Income	$3,900	$46,800
Closing Costs	$8,392	408 Aaron St	$1,300	Taxes	$325.00		Expenses	$2,530	$30,361
Estimated Repairs	$0	410 Aaron St	$1,300	Insurance	$108.33		Cash Flow	$1,370	$16,439
Total Project Cost	$427,972	Unit 4		Water / Sewer	$0.00		Cap Rate	9.91%	
After Repair Value		Unit 5		Trash	$0.00		Cash on Cash RoI	1096%	
		Unit 6		Electric	$0.00		Gross Rent Multiplier	8.97	
Cash to Close (20%)	$1,500	Unit 7		Natural Gas	$0.00		Cash Needed	$9,892	
Loan Amount	$418,080	Unit 8		HOA	$0.00		Yrs to recover	0.60	
Amortization	30	Unit 9		Lawn/Snow	$0.00	0%	Price per unit	$139,860	
Interest Rate	2.75%	Unit 10		Vacancy	$195.00	5%			
Insurance	$1,300	Unit 11		Repairs	$195.00	5%			
Tax	$3,900	Unit 12		CapEx	$0.00	0%			
		Total	$3,900	Total	$2,530.11				

In this scenario, assume that you've purchased your second home and are living with roommates who are paying you rent. From the amount they pay you in rent, you can meet your mortgage payments and break even each month. You're now able to save your BAH of $1,410 plus a cash flow of $1,370 for a total of $2,780 a month or $33,360 a year. You can see how quickly this can snowball if you are diligently saving and living within your means. We'll discuss more of this later in Chapter 7.

Exit Strategy. I like to consider an exit strategy; a vision—with multiple courses of action— that serves as a framework to enable you to make decisions in alignment with your end goal. If you don't have a clear vision of where you want to end up or what your goals are, you will become distracted and distanced from achieving more than a moderate increase in income— or worse, be unprepared for disruptions. Having a clearly defined exit strategy, will enable you to establish the necessary tasks to keep you on course to reaching your goal. As you grow your business, it is imperative to continually gather information about your property's performance, your market, tax laws, and tangential opportunities to protect you from ruin as well as expedite success.

For example, say your original plan was to cash flow $10,000 a month from twenty $500-cash-flowing units. You're currently at $5,000 a month with 10 units but realize one of your properties has had an equity appreciation of over $100,000—due to loan paydown and rising home values in the market. From continuously developing your network, you find out that a local investor is willing to sell his small apartment complex to you before listing it on the MLS. It may serve you better to sell that one property with newly discovered equity appreciation (mentioned above) and utilize a 1031 exchange to purchase his apartment complex.

The latter will produce $4,000 a month in cash flow, thus significantly condensing your original timeline of earning $10,000 a month. Had you not kept your finger on the pulse of tracking the equity you're building up or maintaining and building new relationships, you would have possibly missed an opportunity to shave off four years from the timeline to reach your goal.

Two wealth generators derived from tax laws are the Section 121 exclusion and the 1031 exchange.

Section 121 is the IRS tax code that enables you to exclude up to $250,000 of gain from the sale of your home or up to $500,000 of gain if you file a joint return with your spouse. The condition for this exclusion is that you had to have owned and used the home as a "primary residence" for two of the past five years prior to sale. This would not work if, for example, you lived in a house for two years then moved out of it ten years later—with an eight-year gap of when you lived in it. There is language in this code that is military friendly. Let's say you purchased a home in 2018, lived in it for a year, and then were activated for a deployment or a lengthy TDY; that time away would count towards your two years of required residence in the property. An example of the power of this code is as follows:

Year 1: Purchase a home for $90,000 that needs about $50,000 in repairs.

Year 2: Complete rehab on the home, the house is now worth $185,000

Year 3: Deploy to Afghanistan, totaling nine months away from home.

Year 4: Rent the property, the market has appreciated the home and it is now worth $215,000.

You can sell this home for $215,000. Your tax basis would be a $125,000 gain.

$$(\$215,000) - (\$90,000) = \$125,000 \text{ gain}$$

Assuming that at this point you are in the 22% tax bracket, the amount you would owe Uncle Sam would be:

$$(\$125,000) \times (.22) = \$27,500 \text{ amount owed}$$

Thankfully, due to your foresight and "end in mind" approach, you saw the potential for appreciation with this home the day you bought it and planned your timeline accordingly. This may mean that you spent an additional year living there just so you could qualify for the exclusion in the event the market appreciated how you anticipated. Now, you are $27,500 for the better and can move all that $125,000 into your next project to get yourself that much closer to your goals.

1031 Exchange is the one-for-one swapping of a business or investment property, not personal residence. This rule enables you to shelter gains from a sale by purchasing another property of like-kind exchange qualification. There are two different time limits that you must abide by, otherwise the gain will be taxed. The first one is that within forty-five days of the property sale, you must identify your potential replacement property. The identification must be in writing, signed by you, and delivered to a person involved in the exchange—like the seller of the replacement property or a qualified intermediary.

However, a notice to your attorney, real estate agent, accountant, or similar person—acting as your agent—is not enough. The second timeline is that the purchase of the next property must be concluded by the 180-day mark. Extensions are authorized; but to fully protect yourself, it is recommended to complete your first 1031 exchange with the help of an accountant and an attorney. An example of using 1031 exchanges looks like the following:

- Purchase a 15-unit apartment as an investment property for $1,500,000, with a $500,000 down payment and a mortgage of $1,000,000.
- Enjoy the apartment as a cash-flowing rental for a few years while the loan is being paid down, rents are raising, and the market is appreciating. After some time, you realize you have grown a considerable amount of equity in the property and run the numbers to determine your adjusted basis.

Purchase Price	$1,500,00
PLUS: Acquisition Costs	$10,000
PLUS: Capital Improvements	$65,000
LESS: Depreciation Taken During Ownership	$(400,000)
LESS: Deferred Capital Gains	$ (-0)
EQUALS: Adjusted Tax Basis at Sale	**$1,175,000**

At this point, you've learned that you can sell the property for $2,850,000.

Sales Price	$2,850,000
LESS: Closing Costs	$(50,000)
EQUALS: Net Selling Price	$2,800,000
LESS: Adjusted Tax Basis	$(1,175,000)
EQUALS: Realized Gain	**$1,625,000**

Note: the realized gain is different from cash received from the sale. Assuming the mortgage has been paid down to $800,000, net cash received may look like this:

Sales Price	$2,850,000
LESS: Balance on Mortgage	$(800,000)
LESS: Closing Costs	$(50,000)
EQUALS: Net Cash Received	$2,000,000

Assuming a realized gain of $1,625,000, the sale would likely place you in the highest tax bracket, and your potential tax liabilities may look like this:

Realized Gain	$1,625,000
Federal Capital Gains Tax (20%)	$245,000
Federal Tax on Depreciation Recapture (25%)	$100,000
Affordable Care Act Surtax (3.8%)	$61,750
State Capital Gains Tax (12.3%)	$199,875
Taxes Due (Effective Tax Rate) 37.3%	**$606,625**

By utilizing a 1031 exchange, you may defer the 37.3% in taxes and preserve all of the profit from the sale of the property. This means you have more than $600,000 in additional equity to reinvest!

	With 1031 Exchange	Without 1031 Exchange
Net Proceeds from Sale	$2,000,000	$2,000,000
LESS: Taxes Paid	$ 0	$(606,625)
EQUALS: Equity Available	$2,000,000	$1,393,375

Note: You are not required to reinvest 100% of the sale proceeds into a replacement property. This is known as a "partial exchange." However, the portion of the exchange proceeds that is not reinvested is referred to as "boot" and is subject to tax. However, in order to defer all your capital-gains taxes, the replacement property must have a purchase price and mortgage balance equal to or greater than the property being sold. So, in this example, you would need to find a property for a sale price of greater than $2,850,001 and a mortgage amount greater than $800,001.

Reverse 1031 exchange. A reverse 1031 exchange is basically the opposite of a normal 1031 exchange. The reverse occurs when you find the like-kind replacement property you wish to acquire before selling the property you were originally intending to sell. You are not permitted to own both properties at the same time, so you must utilize an Exchange Accommodation Titleholder (EAT) in the process. They will purchase the replacement property typically in an LLC and then take the title of the property under a Qualified Exchange Accommodation Arrangement (QEAA).

The same 45-day identification period and 180-day exchange period applies to the reverse exchange, with a subtle difference. If the EAT starts the exchange by purchasing the replacement property, then the exchanger must identify which property is to be sold within 45 days. The property you identify to sell must be sold and the replacement property purchased within 180 days. This is a more complicated exchange, so I recommend working with either an experienced CPA or a company that specializes in Reverse 1031 exchanges.

As you can see, the difference between the 1031 and the Section 121 rule is that you are able to keep the cash in a Section 121 transaction. You are unable to touch any cash from the proceeds of a 1031 sale; everything must be rolled into the next property because a 1031 is simply a tax deferment tool. Once you stop rolling into properties with the 1031, your final sale will be taxed. The original deferred gain as well as any additional gain realized since the purchase of the replacement property will be taxed.

Keep in mind as well, these are tax laws that are subject to change annually, so stay informed and utilize these tools to continue to grow your empire as efficiently as possible.

Making the Offer. There are two avenues leading to making an offer: working with a realtor or doing it yourself. Before doing either, I cannot stress enough the importance of understanding an "agreement of sale." I would advise you to read over your state's agreement of sale a dozen times to fully understand all that is involved in purchasing a home, language in the contract, and execution of the deal. After doing this, you will be able to speak with your realtor or seller more intelligently and have more confidence in your ability to work the deal.

Working with a realtor. With a realtor, it will be more of a transactional environment as you're using buyer and seller agents who will filter things in or out to their client. Since you'll be using an intermediary, it's important to vet who will not only be representing you, but also who will be considering deals for you. I like to work with realtors who invest in rental properties themselves. An easy way to determine this, is simply to ask them what their experience is with working for investors and if they have any rentals of their own.

Additionally, you may want to ask some of the following questions to better determine your compatibility with them:

- How long have you been investing in real estate and what types of properties do you own?
- What percentage of your customers are investors?
- How many investor deals have you closed in the past six months?
- What niche do you specialize in? (Flipping homes, multifamily, single family, foreclosures, etc)
- Is being a real estate agent your full-time job?
- Do you have off-market properties or know about upcoming deals to show me before they hit the market?

- What are the comparable homes selling for, renting for, and what is the trend in the specific neighborhood?
- Are there any local upcoming development projects, attractions, or ordinance changes?
- Do they have thick skin and strong negotiating skills?
- Are they transparent in their actions? Having your best interest at heart
- Do they do what they say they will do when they say they will do it?

You can make an absurdly low offer and if the buyer is insulted, it's of no concern to you because they haven't put a face to the name. It's just numbers on a piece of paper. There are some strategies to help fortify your offer even while using a realtor. Things like offering to pay the seller's portion of transfer tax, waiving your inspection, offering above asking price, offering to close in two weeks, etc. Consult with your realtor and learn more about effective tactics in your specific market.

Doing it yourself. Firstly, if you're not going to be working with a realtor, you will want to identify which "title company" you will be working with. Also, it may be in your best interest to use an attorney to review your contract and answer any legal concerns you may have along the way. Do your research ahead of time and develop relationships with both these entities so that when the time comes, you know what to expect. Building Rapport with the Seller:

You only get one chance to make a first impression. When it comes to making deals happen, having a bad first impression can kill the deal before it even gets put together. The importance of building trust and rapport with the seller can't be emphasized enough. When you've established a baseline of trust or likeability, the seller may be more forgiving of your low offering offense. The keys to avoiding burning rapport is:

Don't be the first to name a price. If you can structure the conversation such that it naturally leads to the seller giving you the number first without them realizing what you're doing, you've cracked the code on clever and should feel proud. This also gives you a framework to navigate in. You should be having this dialogue with several numbers already in mind, anticipating what they may say and being able to adjust fire as necessary.

Have multiple price points identified. I recommend having three or four specific dollar amounts in mind and knowing what your return on investment (ROI) is with each one. This becomes more important for properties you're looking to flip than rentals because typically the price for rentals won't vary as significantly as homes in distress once they're renovated. Valuation of rentals is well contained as it is based on the gross revenue generated through rents paid. When you look at it a step further, you'll realize that if interest rates are at 3%, you can pay an extra

$10,000 for the property, and it only decreases your monthly cash flow by roughly thirty dollars. Likewise, if you get the property for $10,000 less—from a cash flow perspective—it only annualizes to $360 more in income.

An example of having multiple price points identified is in the following. Say you're going to purchase a distressed property to flip. You find it listed on craigslist for $135,000. After looking through the pictures and running comparable sales, you estimate that it should be worth $185,000 after about $40,000 worth of rehab and carrying costs. With this information, you can set up a spreadsheet to determine what price points will dictate which cash profit or percentage returned on your purchase price. For flip properties, I don't pursue deals unless they have at least a 25% ROI. Using that as the baseline, I would have the following numbers in my head ready for when I converse with the property owner.

25% ROI - $116,000 Purchase Price - $29,000 Profit
35% ROI - $107,500 Purchase Price - $37,500 Profit
40% ROI - $103,500 Purchase Price - $41,500 Profit
50% ROI - $96,500 Purchase Price - $48,500 Profit
75% ROI - $83,000 Purchase Price - $62,000 Profit

When it comes time to talk price, always lead with a specific number. In this case, I would use $83,167 and say something like the following:

"I appreciate you taking the time to show me around the house, and I've run the numbers on my spreadsheet which computes an optimum purchase price for my criteria. I'm not looking to insult you, but I just want to voice that—though you're asking $135,000—for the costs I'm expecting to incur to restore the beauty of this property, I would like to purchase this property for $83,167. Is that number anywhere near the mark of what you find reasonable?"

Just wait and let that linger and watch for their response. If you find that the seller has become upset with that offer, don't let it ruin the moment. Quickly adapt—put the ball back in their court—and kindly let them know that it's just an optimal computing solution, and you understand it comes in low because it's built to protect you (the buyer) from risk. You're not a computer, however, and do value creating an optimal resolution for both parties. That's why you're able to close in two weeks or use whatever value proposition you have. Now comes the framework shift and having them tell you where their head is at. They may say that, given the fact that you can close in two weeks, they would be willing to discuss somewhere in the $100,000 range. Well, you're prepared for this because you know that $103,500 would put you at a $41,500 profit. Give them a little win and say yes, I think the $100,000 range is reasonable, how is $101,500?

Have multiple offer adaptions available. Every seller has a unique situation. Your competitive advantage is discovering what their motivating factor is and appeal to that. In addition to the standard "pay for asking price" using a conventional loan, here are some alternative options to consider based on the motivating factors:

Quick exit. Some are in a rush to get out of the house as quickly as possible for whatever reason and would take a significant price reduction if you could pay cash and close quickly. Oftentimes, these sellers have inherited the property, are settling through a divorce, are relocating, are facing foreclosure, or had a failed business venture. These situations will afford you the most leverage in negotiating the lowest price. You may even find that working with a "hard money lender" or gathering the funds from your network to purchase it can save you tens of thousands of dollars by accommodating the seller's situation.

Seller financing. Others are wanting to maximize their sale without incurring a significant tax burden. This situation opens the door for seller financing that works best with sellers who have paid off the mortgage on the property or have a significant amount of equity. Here, you enter an agreement wherein the seller essentially acts like the lender, and you pay them directly without involving a bank. You will negotiate a down payment and the terms of the sale more creatively than traditional financing.

The seller may only owe $10,000 on their mortgage, so you could do a $10,000 down payment to free them of their mortgage obligation and create your own interest and amortization schedule—with or without a balloon payment after a certain number of years. The seller will still be paying taxes on the sale of the home; however, it is distributed into smaller installments over the years that they will be able to better manage within their tax strategy. It's a win-win situation because if you default on payments, they take the house back; but if you're able to pay them consistently, they are receiving monthly cash flow with no tenant headaches, and you are purchasing a property without having to take out a loan. In this manner, you assume all responsibility for the property. Another benefit is that there are significantly fewer closing costs incurred with this type of transaction.

Offer over asking price. This can be beneficial when utilizing bank financing. If you're getting the property at a discount, many times you can increase the purchase price and have the seller contribute more towards closing costs, so it will lessen the amount of out-of-pocket cash for you and net them the same profit. For example, if you are purchasing a multifamily property that was listed for $300,000, but you know it should appraise for $320,000, you can agree upon a $315,000 sale price and have the seller cover your closing costs, so they still net a $300,000 sale. Now, you're able to keep that $15,000 worth of closing costs in cash, and it is amortized over the period of your loan. It is totally appraisal dependent, so you can make final adjustments after the appraisal comes back.

Closing costs. Even if you feel that the property is worth what is being asked or still more, let your initial offer be a little less and include language that states you will pay all the closing costs and fees with the transaction. If the seller counters for full asking price, say you'll gladly pay the full asking price if they pay all the closing costs. In this scenario, you're either buying the property at a discount or able to purchase with less money down.

Finally, always protect yourself (the buyer):

Include contingent language. Always incorporate at least one contingency in your contract to protect yourself if during the discovery period, you uncover something that significantly alters the value of the deal. You can waive your right to inspection but include a clause that states, "purchase is subject to satisfactory approval of the general contractor or electrician." You don't need a good reason other than the fact that it wasn't satisfactory to you, so you are no longer obligated to the deal. Find a reason that is relevant to the condition of the home. If a seller reads a contract that has twenty different contingencies, it will weaken their confidence in your offer and weaken your negotiating position.

Don't be afraid to walk away. After all the hours and headaches involved with completing this deal, do not allow your emotional investment to outweigh the numbers and logic of the situation. If at some point along the way you discover this deal no longer meets your criteria or is not a financially beneficial decision, walk away. The numbers never lie and there will always be more deals. Don't tie yourself into a bad deal just because you've spent a couple hundred bucks and untold hours trying to make it work. You'll thank yourself in the long run. You may even find that the seller is needy to sell, and you can renegotiate under terms that better serve your goals.

Negotiation. There are hundreds of books written on negotiation. This section will just cover the basics and some techniques that I've personally used or witnessed in use that were effective. Some of the principles from the "Making the Offer" section (above) will overlap, so apply accordingly. Just like Valentine's Day, if it's only something you're doing once a year, you're not going to be very good at it. Negotiating is a perishable skill set that initially should be practiced daily on a smaller scale until you build up the expertise to take to higher stakes. At the end of the book, there will be a list of recommended reading that will include several great books on negotiating.

The first and most crucial skill to develop for successful negotiating is your ability to actively listen to someone. This is not something you read about and become an expert on immediately the next day; it is a habit and practice that only comes from active use. A great active listener can take in not only the words being said but the inflection of that person's voice and body language to fully grasp the message being communicated.

According to an article in Psychology Today, "the belief is that 55% of communication is body language, 38% is the tone of voice, and 7% is the actual words spoken." You may be hearing language from someone that is telling you one thing, but the way they deliver it may indicate there is some form of conflict or motivation behind what they're telling you. At the end of the day, everyone wants to feel respected, heard, and appreciated. The more you can facilitate those sentiments, the further down the negotiating line you will be able to take them. Emotions and how people perceive you and the situation carry much more impact than what may seem completely logical and rational.

When people become emotional, they can become irrational, which then turns into an inability to listen. When people can't or won't listen, they can't be persuaded. Your responsibility is to never let it get that far.

One way to maintain active listening and avoid tense emotions is to use a technique known as "mirroring." This is simply repeating some of the key words the other person said to show them that you are listening and understand them. Anybody can sit and nod their head until the other person has finished speaking. Nobody knows what's going on in your gray matter if you're just giving north-souths for ten minutes straight. Emphasizing their key points or— with a short sentence—paraphrasing what they last said, lets them know you're attentive and seeking to understand them.

This is where you begin to make your money in laying the framework for negotiating. Using the mirroring technique, you should be attentive enough to realize what is not being said and start to tease that out of them. It may be that they are selling the house because of a divorce and are in over their head with stress and emotions, and this house is such a burden to them that they can't wait to get out of it. With that knowledge, you can pivot the conversation to how you can make this a worry-free transaction for them.

Talk about whatever value you may be adding to this deal such as a quick closing time, flexing around their schedule, and even taking it a step further to see if there's a genuine way you can help them—like offering to help move their stuff out of the property. Empathy is a powerful tool in influencing others, just be sure to come across as genuine. If your words aren't in line with your intentions, people can smell the inconsistency a mile away and perceive you as suspicious.

Now that you've been listening to them and mirroring their sentiments, you've certainly found material to work with in enabling more negotiation. An interesting technique that has yielded me tremendous success is incorporating the seller in the solution. You want to make it seem like you're working together, for the best of both parties, by continuously asking them variations of "how." People become emotionally invested in finding collaborative solutions and naturally want to help others.

By continuously asking them variations of "how"— such as, "how can we make this work?" or "how are we making this a win-win situation for each other?", you will get significantly more buy-in from them and hopefully a mutually beneficial deal. The important piece of the puzzle here is to discover how much is being left on the table. In my first sales job, the general manager often incorporated negotiation role plays into our quarterly conferences. An example of one I found particularly useful is described below.

Negotiation Role Play Exercise

Employee A will play the part of a carpenter in need of work to pay this month's bills. Employee B will play the part of the homeowner looking to remodel their kitchen. Employee A needs $2,500 to pay his bills and hasn't had work in a few weeks. Employee B has set a budget for $10,000 to remodel the kitchen but has no idea how much it could cost. The employees don't know about each other's financial situations and are instructed to have a conversation to negotiate the best possible deal. When I played, I believe I was able to get the job down to $3,000 and my coworker was shocked to find that I would have been willing to spend $10,000.

I was able to do this because of my line of questioning and rapport building with the carpenter. I sought first to relate to them on a human-to-human basis by finding common ground. We both enjoyed hunting and were looking forward to the upcoming white-tailed-deer season. Making that human connection builds positive momentum in your favor as you are the one controlling the framework. We moved past the initial pressures and awkwardness of the arrangement and built a foundation on common ground that I intended to leverage for my series of indirect questioning.

For example, I asked if he had any hunting trips planned for the upcoming season to which he admitted that money was tight, and he would be unable to afford one. Reading between the lines, I could see that since money was tight for him, he would be more flexible in terms of pricing for the job because he needed the work. It is a great tactic to use this type of indirect questioning where the person you are talking to answers out of genuineness, and you can use the information gleaned to your advantage without them even realizing what they gave you. Additionally, I bolstered my framework by talking about how multiple contractors were coming in and out with quotes for me. They were ranging from very cheap to very expensive, but my most important consideration was the price—not necessarily the amount of time the work took to complete.

I then searched for ways to alleviate pain for him to make him more willing to yield to my terms. Understanding that money was tight, I proposed two ideas. The first, to pay him in full upfront at a discounted rate today. This played on the emotion of the need for cash and my willingness to pay in full and pay now. Second, allow him to work on my kitchen on the side in addition to other jobs he may have, also at a discounted rate. This spoke to my flexibility and understanding that he needs work; so, if he was motivated enough to be working two jobs, the opportunity was there to provide the income for him.

Most importantly, I made him speak the first number so I could pivot from that number according to what I had in mind. Fortunately, the first number he suggested was $3,000. Sometimes it's most prudent to understand you have a good deal and simply keep your mouth closed and go with it. Since we had built good rapport, and the price he suggested was only 30% of my budget, I knew I had a good deal.

I did not wish to squeeze out every last penny from him so that I could preserve the relationship for potential future use. When negotiating, while it is ideal to always strive for a win-win scenario, you need to make sure all the options you suggest are at least wins for yourself—with varying levels of wins for the other party. This way, whichever option they select, you have already determined it to be a good opportunity for yourself and can come to an agreement on the spot. This is a fun exercise that demonstrates all the key points in negotiating. Specifically, the fact that there is always money left on the table and you may just be two questions away from taking a good deal to a great deal.

Relevant to the previous story, there's typically three rounds on average for most negotiations. Simply having one dialogue exchange could certainly lead to a significant amount of money being left on the table, yet too much back-and-forth could cause a loss of credibility and kill the deal. This is when the power of the "pause" comes into play. You want to get to a stage in your negotiating career where you can frame the conversation so that they will be the ones to give the first price. In negotiating, whoever says the price first loses. This is true because you'll never really know just how far their price range may have been unless they verbalized it. Once verbalized, you can begin to intuitively estimate how far you can stretch them.

Bank-on-it Tip #4:

In my experience, I have found that I can get away with initially offering about 70% of my purchase price point.

I like to think of this as anchoring them down to the worst-for-them scenario and seeing what their verbal and nonverbal language is telling me. Psychologically, they want to feel that they were able to use their negotiating skills and protect themselves from being raked over the coals. Give them that. For your next offer, come up 20% and reassess the situation. Another technique to include here would be asking for something unrelated as part of your concession. Find ways to trade ones for tens; that is, giving up something of low importance for you, to gain something of higher importance. Beforehand, you should identify parts of the deal that you must have and parts that aren't as important to you. For example, here is a list of seller concessions to keep in mind for negotiation:

- Payment of the VA funding fee.
- Prepayment of property taxes and insurance.
- Gifts such as a tv, microwave, fridge, stove, etc.
- Payment of extra points to provide permanent interest rate buydowns.
- Provision of escrowed funds to provide temporary interest rate buydowns.

- Payoff of credit card balances or judgments on behalf of the buyer.

Note: Under VA guidelines, the seller cannot offer concessions which go beyond 4% of the property value.

After you've come up 20% and, if need be, continue to increase your offer, do so in smaller increments. For example, in the next round, come up 10% and then if needed, 5%; all the while maintaining your empathy and frame-control to make them feel like they are in control and making a great deal. Realistically, you were satisfied to buy it at your 100% price point; but you are realizing a better deal, the deeper you get into percentages.

It will be important for you to do your due diligence beforehand and come to the conversation prepared with numbers and non-priced items in mind for increased negotiating power.

However, also keep in mind the phase of the market. If inventory is flying off the shelves, sellers know their product is in demand and will have less patience for your antics. On the flip side, if it's a buyer's market, time is on your side—and you can use that as a great form of leverage. Have clearly defined objectives as you navigate your negotiation process and strive to meet those goals, anything else is of marginal importance.

Check on Learning:

1. Where can you download the Deal Analysis Spreadsheet?

- www.thecashflowcommando.com

2. What is cash flow?

- The cash coming into your pocket each month. Income - expenses.

3. What is the Cap Rate formula?

- Net operating income divided by the property's value. (NOI / Value = Cap Rate %)

4. What is the Cash on Cash Return on Investment formula?

- Net cash flow divided by down payment cost. (CF / DP = CoC ROI)

5. What is the Gross Rent Multiplier formula?

- Price of the home divided by the rent. (Value / Rent = GRM)

6. What is an Exit Strategy?

- A vision that encompasses multiple courses of actions which serves as a framework to enable you to make decisions in alignment with your end goal.

7. What are two tax options to consider when exiting a property?

- IRS Section 121 and the 1031 Exchange

8. List some tactics for making an offer:

- Build Rapport

- Don't be the first to name a price

- Have multiple price points identified

- Have multiple offer adaptions available

- Try to close quickly

- If possible, utilize seller financing

- Offer over asking

- Share closing costs

- Include contingent language

Chapter 7

SYSTEMS & MANAGEMENT

About Property Management. In the real estate game, the two factors affecting your cash flow are how high your rent is and how low your expenses are. The greater the disparity between these two-line items, the larger your pile of cash will be each month. Effective property management will enable you to control your expenses and, with good enough service, justify higher rent.

For your first several properties, I recommend managing them yourself unless you are stationed overseas investing in the United States or have long-distance rentals. Managing your own properties presents a new set of challenges for you to learn and grow from—but can also save you a lot of money. You may come to realize that investing in real estate is not for you after managing just one property, or you simply do not have the time or desire to manage them yourself and then decide to hire out. On the other hand, you may realize that managing your own properties, when done effectively, doesn't really require that much mental bandwidth or time. As a very general rule of thumb, I typically advise that once you're around fifty units in your portfolio, you may find it more beneficial to hire a property management company. This way, less of your time is spent reacting to tenants and better served putting together larger deals.

When you manage your own properties, you will become intimately acquainted with each of the unique quirks your properties have and general issues that may arise from their location or tenant demographic. This knowledge is important to better vet a property management company to run the property to your liking when you've already been there and done that. Improper management can ruin what was once a low-hassle, high-earning property.

Coming back to the story I mentioned in Chapter 5, my first property was a duplex in a college town. I was living in one half and renting the other. Once I moved out, I continued to manage the property myself and lived about five miles away. Whenever there were issues, I would respond immediately and go to the property for every one of these issues, big or small. I had not trained my tenants effectively, and they were often eating up my time and resources unnecessarily. During this period, I was also scheduled for a two-month pre-deployment training, followed by a six-month trip. I knew I wasn't going to have consistent

Wi-Fi access to maintain the property myself, so I began reaching out to property management companies. Through having a good network in the area, I found a guy—who was a landlord himself—that managed over twenty units in the same area and was willing to manage mine while I was gone. We discussed expectations, communication, and how we would move forward. Everything was going great for the first few months until he was incarcerated for an altogether unrelated incident.

Now, I'm overseas and eight hours ahead with limited Wi-Fi capacity to do research, make calls, and hire an actual company for the first time. This is where mistakes were made. Since I was in a time crunch and didn't have the luxury to see how the different companies operated, I had to take their word for it— trust what they were telling me and decide based on intuition. My property was relatively low-maintenance. The only thing looming on the horizon was that a tenant was due to move out within a couple months, so a new tenant would need to be installed. After speaking with three management companies, I decided to go with the one that had responded to my calls and emails in the timeliest manner. In addition, they had what appeared to be lower fees. They charged seventy dollars per unit for management, one month's rent as the leasing fee, and a 15% fee on top of service calls. Their pricing seemed very reasonable so— without much hesitation—I went with them. The first month everything was fine; they collected the rent and, at the end of the month, sent me a statement with my money (minus their $140)—great.

The next month and every month thereafter, it seemed there was a new issue at the property that required service, and their 15% service fees started to really add up. By now, the aforesaid unit had become vacant and three months later, still no tenant had been installed. The market rate was between $1,600–$1,800 monthly for this unit. Even with listing it at $1,600 (though it was previously rented for $1,800), they were still unable to place a tenant. They suggested that if I lowered my rate to $1,200, they were confident that they could place a tenant. This was another fork in the road for my decision-making. Do I take the negative $400–$600 a month hit to at least get someone in there, or do I keep holding out in hopes of them finding a tenant to pay my desired rate? I looked over how much I was spending on property management and how it affected my cash flow.

Over the course of a year (between fees, service calls, and unit assessments), they had cost me almost 30% of my cash flow. I took a step back to reevaluate my strategy with this property and, after some research, found that the property had appraised $100,000 over what I paid for it. Additionally, I learned that I would be undergoing a Permanent Change of Station (PCS) and realized I would most likely need to use a property manager there for the foreseeable future.

After analyzing cash flow projections for the future with this management company in place and realizing what the sale of the home would enable me to do in my new location, I decided to sell the house. It was a blessing in disguise that one unit was vacant because, oftentimes, multifamily homes are more marketable when one unit is empty. This is because people looking to utilize a VA Loan or Federal Housing Administration (FHA) first-time home buyer loan need to be considered owner occupants, so they can qualify for those low or no-money-down loan products. Shortly after listing the property, I was able to close the sale, take those profits, and move them into my next deal.

I've taken away multiple lessons learned from this situation and will gladly pass them on to you.

Lesson 1: As mentioned earlier, you need to account for property management in your deal analysis so that when or if the time comes to utilize one, you know what to expect in terms of cash flow. If it's not in your plan to use a property manager for several years or you end up not needing one, then the money that would be allocated to them in your analysis is simply more cash in your pocket each month. However, if you know you will need to use a property manager and this service makes the property cash flow negative, it may not be in your best interest to continue with the purchase of the property unless you have another strategy in mind for how you will be maximizing the potential of this asset.

Lesson 2: The best decisions are rarely made impulsively or under a time crunch. Take the time to evaluate several companies before needing them, so you can establish a baseline of what to expect and who you would want to work with. You can ask around in your local network if anyone has heard good or bad reviews about them as well. This way, if you do need to use one, you already have a list to reference and can feel more comfortable selecting whoever fits your needs best. I should have continued to reach out to management companies even after hiring my initial guy, so I could have a backup already in mind. It is not uncommon to go through a few companies until you find the one that works best for you.

Lesson 3: Establish the framework with the company. Typically, they'll require you to leave them money in escrow for small repairs and work required that is under a certain dollar threshold. This is so they won't have to bother contacting you about it, and they'll just deduct the difference from your monthly rent. I did not explicitly cover which repairs or to what extent I wanted to be consulted on before having them send their handyman. In consequence, there were oftentimes issues where they did things I wouldn't have agreed upon. For example, they charged me $115 to get a key out of a lockbox at the property to make themselves a copy instead of asking me first if I had one that I could mail to them, which I did and could have for fifty cents.

One of the positives I take away from this company was the fact that ninety days prior to tenant turnover, they conduct an inspection on the property to assess what may need to be repaired during the transition and offer you three different quotes for the job. I've since carried this with me.

 Bank-on-it Tip #5:

For each unit I have that will soon undergo turnover, I conduct a ninety-day inspection. This can be good for the tenant as well because instead of having to subtract the cost from their security deposit, you can give them a chance to fix whatever their issue may be and let them walk away with most of their deposit—plus, you have less to repair.

After this experience, I came up with a few principles to better manage my tenants. If you can apply these basic principles, you will cut your number of headaches in half and realize that you can manage a much larger portfolio before resorting to a property management company.

Property Management Principles:
1. Leadership
2. Timeliness
3. Consistency
4. Integrity
5. Respect
6. Cleanliness
7. Discernment

Let's go over these principles more in depth.

1. Leadership: The Army's definition of leadership is, "...the activity of influencing people by providing purpose, direction, and motivation to accomplish the mission and improve the organization." In this case, the organization is your rental business. The mission is to grow that business. The direction is for your tenants to pay on time, respect your property, and alert you of repairs needed in a timely manner. As the landlord, you're already placed in a framework of authority. It is up to you to embody that authority and proactively manage your tenants because if you don't, they will be managing you. People can be difficult and unpredictable; therefore, landlording is a unique challenge and art. It is your responsibility to better understand human beings and how to motivate and influence them so that when you have a tenant giving you a difficult time, you can come up with a proper solution.

In the military, there are several chains of command providing a wide variety of influence and experiences. Some provide toxic environments that make you want to do less and be less because of their lack of leadership or interpersonal skills. Others motivate you to go to hell and back for them and pull difficult duty with a smile on your face because you know they've got your back and will fight for you. You need to instill that same type of confidence into your tenants.

Since it's not a large warfighting organization, it should be that much easier to build a similar rapport with your tenants. For example, treating people like people. Oftentimes, landlords have a stereotype for being extremely cheap, inconsiderate, or even unavailable. This is how a toxic environment is created. When a tenant feels like you don't have their best interest in mind, don't return their calls, or plainly write them off, they won't be motivated to take care of and respect your property.

This could also manifest into late payments, unnecessary damage to units, and even damage to your reputation in the community. Inversely, if your tenant feels valued and can see that you care for your property and treat them with dignity and respect, they will be most likely to pay on time or renew leases with you. Additionally, they'll take a vested interest in the property and may call you as a heads-up about other issues arising with neighboring units, or they will be proactive in calling you if they can't make the rent that month to find a way to set up a payment plan.

Little things can go a long way. I typically send my tenants Christmas cards with a ten-dollar gift card to Dunkin Donuts, Amazon, or something of equal value. I use verbiage in my letters that show how much I appreciate the fact that they're great tenants because they pay on time and respect my property, and I acknowledge that I see this and want to reward it with this gesture. Ninety percent of the people that received those letters gave me a call or sent me a text and were so grateful for just a little ten-dollar gift because no previous landlord had done anything like that for them. I knew I had earned their respect already by providing timely repairs, but this was a move that sustained the influence I had to make them "want" to take care of the properties and pay on time because they like me. People will do more for you if they like you or feel that you have their back. This is just one way of showing that.

2. *Timeliness:* There's a difference between "punctuality" and "timeliness" and that difference is that punctuality is the habit of always being on time, where timeliness is something happening at the appropriate time. When it comes to managing rental properties, for your own sanity, it is more important to be *timely* than *punctual*. This means that if a tenant has clogged a toilet at 11:00 p.m. and calls you, you do not need to drop what you're doing to drive down

there and fix it or pay an emergency rate for a repairman—unless, of course, it's flooding your unit. They clogged the toilet; they can be the ones to go to Walmart and buy the drain snake. You should have a system in place that if a tenant calls after a certain time, they get a prerecorded message and information of whom to contact in the event of an emergency.

Describe what an emergency is in your lease or in the message. If it is anything else, it can wait until reasonable hours the next day. Otherwise, once you develop the habit of going there for every phone call, the tenants will assume you have the time and capacity to come whenever they call. This is bad training of tenants. You need to establish that you will respond to their inquiry in a timely manner, however, you need to also identify the priority of the situation and adjust accordingly. Strive to be quick to respond yet timely to repair.

3. Consistency: Doing what you say you'll do. This may be one of the most common mistakes landlords of all portfolio sizes make, and people in general for that matter. There is no quicker way to lose respect or credibility than to be known as a person who doesn't live up to their word. Oftentimes, it only takes one time for you to say you were going to do something and not follow through for the dynamic to change. Empty threats and empty promises fall into this principle equally. Don't tell a tenant you'll be evicting them and not follow through because when they don't get the eviction notice, they'll realize that you're not a person of your word and most likely will not be quick to pursue eviction. This will make them comfortable with paying late and become a habitual non-payer. Thus, your lack of action creates opportunity for a worse reaction. Tenants will start losing respect for you and the property, and they will begin to walk all over you because you're not providing that clear leadership nor being consistent with them. Likewise, if you say you'll get something repaired, get it repaired. Don't allow feelings of uncertainty and resentment to fester within your tenant. Happy tenants pay on time and respect your property. Doubtful ones don't.

4. *Integrity:* Do what is right, legally and morally, even when no one is looking. Integrity is one of the foundational qualities necessary for enduring success. You can lie, cheat, and steal your way to the top, but it is not sustainable nor recommended. You're only as good as your word and once that becomes meaningless, you will quickly find out that people will not want to work with you or trust you with anything. There are countless ways integrity works its way into landlording, but two of the most important scenarios cover working with your contractors and your tenants. For tenants, this means honoring your lease and expectations according to how you wrote them. You have an obligation to follow your state's requirements in terms of housing laws, discrimination policies, rent

raises, and eviction. For contractors, don't burn them or go back on your word to save a couple bucks. There is an ever-decreasing amount of skilled labor in the workplace and bad gas travels fast in a small town. I've seen landlords, too many times, cut bad checks or try to find ways out of paying agreed-upon fees for service. Your properties and business can soon become blacklisted amongst contractors, which will force you to make all your own repairs or pay top dollar to larger businesses for your needs.

5. *Respect:* When you give and show respect to yourself and other people, it automatically reflects in your own life. Practicing respect allows you to have better connections with people. When people feel respected and understood, you lay the groundwork for successful communication and relationships. Though real estate investing may seem transactional on spreadsheets, it's a human business and you need to practice being a good human.

An environment of mutual respect enables the option to maintain peace in that environment. Tenants that respect you will in turn be most likely to respect your property—and that's the name of the game. You don't want to be a jerk and have tenants loathe interacting with you because it will reflect on the care they give to your asset.

6. *Cleanliness:* There's no excuse to be a slumlord no matter which asset class you invest in. It's your duty to provide a safe and clean environment for the

people living in your properties. When you take the effort to maintain cleanliness, you can demand the same from your tenants, and it becomes an expectation for them to follow. Just like with your body, a disheveled outward appearance can tell a lot about what's inside.

A filthy and distraught-looking rental property reflects on the owner and the respect or pride they have for themselves. This translates to when your units require township inspections. Like the old "Pine-Sol" trick in cleaning your basic-training bays, if it smells clean, typically the drill sergeants are less nitpicky because they can tell you put in the effort to clean.

Likewise, if your property is disgusting and appears unkempt, it gives the inspector more incentive to be more nitpicky in their requirements to bring your unit to satisfactory levels. Oftentimes, if the property looks like it is being maintained and generally clean, they'll be more willing to let some things slide because they can tell you put in the effort to provide safe and reasonable housing environments for your tenants.

7. *Discernment:* This is something you will gain by experience as you become a more sophisticated investor. For example, when a tenant calls you about their clogged shower drain, learn to ask questions before rushing over there to repair it. Inform the tenant that it is your responsibility to make timely repairs and cover the costs unless it is tenant induced.

If you send your plumber over there to fix their drain and find Barbie dolls lodged into said drain, the tenant is then liable to pay for the repair because you did not put a Barbie doll in the drain to cause this issue.

Typically, when you have this conversation prior to sending a repairman out, you'll find that the tenant quickly finds a way to remedy the problem and thus saves you the time and money of fixing it. In another situation, you may find that there was a miscommunication between you and a contractor, and the contractor is asking you to pay for some materials that were not discussed in the scope of the work.

Learning to pick your battles by asking yourself what is reasonable will yield dividends. It may be that the contractor is only asking for an extra fifty dollars, so you decide to meet him in the middle because you don't want to ruin the relationship and be able to work with them in the future. Moreover, you could find that he's asking for 50% more than what was quoted, and his justification is unreasonable—so you can have confidence in your decision of how to proceed.

Planning Ahead. Like with your due diligence and deal analysis, you want to take an "end in mind" approach. This starts with incorporating a property management fee in your deal analysis if down the road you may utilize such a service. Once accounted for, you can begin to think long term as it pertains to managing your portfolio. Ask yourself the following questions:

- Do I have any deployments coming up? When? For how long?
- Will I be in any field-training exercises without cell phone or computer access?
- When is my next Permanent Change of Station (PCS)? Where?
- When do I plan to vacation or take a trip with limited cell access?
- Where am I with my portfolio today and where do I want to be with it in three, five, or ten years down the road?

With answers to these questions, you'll be able to look at a calendar and start identifying blocked-off dates where you'll need property management assistance. The earlier you can prepare, the better served you will be to ensure a seamless transition for that period. An ounce of prevention is worth more than a pound of the cure in this instance. You will find that it may be a good time, several weeks out from your deployment or PCS, to walk through your properties and identify any upcoming repairs that may need to be addressed while you're gone and begin scheduling them.

Talk with your tenants and find out if there are any smaller issues that they have been putting up with but not mentioning to you that could possibly result in a larger problem if not addressed. Let your tenants know that you will be unreachable or require a different means of communication (Signal/WhatsApp/Google Voice/Email).

- Give them direction as to how you will navigate the changes and what they can expect. Firstly, you want to think deeply and cover all your bases so when you have the conversation with them, you will readily have answers to the questions they may raise. Things such as:
- What to do if the unit needs repairs.
- How to contact for late rent.
- Where to send the rent payment.
- How to proceed with the move out (turnover) process.
- How to proceed with snow removal or lawn maintenance.
- How to proceed with utility service installation or discontinuance.

I found that in preparing myself for going weeks without phone or computer access, I needed to create a Standard Operating Procedure (SOP) binder and have someone be my stand-in point of contact and decision-maker. You will need to identify such a person whether it be someone you trust or someone in a trustworthy capacity that you can pay to handle your affairs while you're inaccessible.

The Cash Flow Commando Website

For your benefit, I've repackaged my personal SOPs into a fillable template eBook, available for purchase online at *The Cash Flow Commando* website. You may tweak them however you need to, just understand that the most important thing is to give them a framework to operate in that enables them to make the most reasonable decisions that align with your interests while you're gone. Thoroughly discuss your SOPs with them and make them as simple as possible to reference, digest, and act upon.

 Bank-on-it Tip #6:

The intent of the SOP binder is to function like a staff duty binder, meaning anyone can refer to it and solve 95% of their problems from reading it.

If having a scenario like this for yourself is not an option, consult some property management companies and see if they can be flexible in their terms to accommodate your unique position. Typically, they'll only want to do business on yearly terms because it's not profitable for them to go through the onboarding process and administrative work to only manage your property for a few weeks or months—so be willing to negotiate within this framework.

Apps and Tools. As you grow in your investing career and continue to increase your portfolio, you will quickly realize that a basic notepad or excel spreadsheet will no longer be the most effective means for managing your assets. It will become too much to track neatly and in a simple, straightforward, and organized fashion. If you can systemize something, you can automate something. Once you can automate aspects of your business, it can significantly reduce the time burden required for those tasks.

To be a successful real estate investor, you need to treat it like a business. As businesses grow, their infrastructure should be growing to keep up with their volume. There is a difference between growing a business and scaling a business. Growing a business refers to increasing revenue as a result of business activities. Things like increased number of employees, locations, and clients served relate to growth of revenue.

All these things require a lot of resources to sustain constant, linear growth. Scaling a business requires processes, systems, and resourcefulness (as opposed to acquiring more resources). Scaling differs from growth in that scaling is when revenue can increase without a significant increment in resources or expenses. For example, you own properties in a region that gets annual snowfall. There is a storm approaching, and you need to call your tenants to inform them to move their vehicles so that your plow service can come by and plow the parking lot. Instead of making ten phone calls taking anywhere from ten to twenty minutes, you can take the time to make one prerecorded message and have it sent to all those tenants at once. There isn't a specific path to how to scale your business as everyone has their own unique portfolio composition and preferences, but the more ways you can find to scale, the quicker and more effective your growth will become.

For this reason, many companies have developed software to assist in this multi-billion-dollar industry that is property management. Depending on what stage you are in with your investment career, more of the following factors will apply to you, so you should have a mindset of growth and look to what you will need as you are achieving your goals.

Factors to consider in selecting a property management software:

- *Management of property maintenance.* Look for collaborative software that enables communication from the tenant to submit maintenance requests. Once alerted, you or your maintenance personnel will be able to schedule, track, and document them with photographs of job completed and receipts for your expenses.
- *Integration with other solutions.* Enable a one-stop shop element that will significantly reduce time and resources. For example, the ability to link with accounting software or listing sites (e.g.,

MLS). You should have an application that allows you to communicate with an external customer-relationship management software or an application with its own internal solution. A customer-relationship management software enables you to store customer information, notes, emails, and phone call history—as well as calendar reminders and auto-generated emails based on your desired timelines.

- *Payment Collection.* One of the most critical aspects is to be able to receive rent securely and electronically. You want to make it as easy as possible for tenants to pay their rent on time and without much of a convenience fee. Equally important, the application you choose for this service should have a method to reimburse tenants for security deposits, repairs, overpayment, etc.
- *Vacancy management.* A very useful tool is the ability to track leases on a calendar and set reminders to conduct follow-up phone calls or unit inspections with tenants that have upcoming lease expirations.
- *Tenant Screening.* Most applications offer some form of tenant screening service or partnership with a third party. The less work on your end in having to run background checks and make phone calls, the more productive you will be. Understand the tenant screening process and if it fits your requirements. You may simply receive an

immediate "Yes/No" from the software application if they meet your predefined criteria. From here, you only need to call previous landlords to confirm vetting.

- *Other.* If you have partners or outside investors, you may want to consider features that include "report generation" for profit and expense tracking, real time data syncing, and built-in accounting software.

How to decide which platform to purchase. Evaluate where you stand today. How many units are you managing? How much time are you spending managing these properties? Would you value a less time-intensive, more streamlined approach to running this business? Once you've answered those basic questions, you can begin to identify which services are most beneficial to you, based on where you are at today. You may only have five units and are looking for a more organized way to collect rent and screen tenants for those units. There's software out there that does simply that, for free.

On the other hand, maybe you have thirty-five units of a wide variety and want to streamline your efforts, so you need a software that serves all the factors listed above. Nonetheless, you may find whatever system you're currently utilizing is what works best for you, and that's fine. The intent is to maximize your efficiency and utility. Research the list of applications below; see which interface you prefer the most and which price points align with your budget. Also, consider how quickly you may be growing and the direction your portfolio will be taking to see if the platform is only for temporary use or if it has the potential to scale with you.

List of Property Management Applications:

123Landlord
AccuRently
Acturent
Alcalo
Avail.co
AppFolio
Beaver
Buildium
Burbz
Caretaker
CondoControlCentral

Cozy.co
Decorus for Sage
DIY
RealEstateSolutions
EasyRent
Hemlane
Housters
iRealty
Landlordy
ManageGo
NowRenting

Payrent
PropertyBoss
Property
Boulevard
Property Matrix
Propertyware
Property Vista
PropertyZar
Re-Leased
RentalIncomeExpense
Rentalutions

Rentec Direct
Rentigo
Rent Manager
RentPost
RentPrep
Renttropolis
RentRedi
Tracxn
SimplifyEm
SparkRental
Tellus

TenantCloud
Tenant Ledger
TrueRent
TurboTenant
UnitConnect
Unitdash
Wave
Community
Yardi
Ziprent
Zuby App
Zumper

Hiring a Property Management Company. There comes a point when it only makes sense to hire a property management company. If you are a long-distance investor, are becoming too distracted from your main job, have no desire to build your own management company, or simply have no desire to continue to manage the property yourself, then hiring out is absolutely the right decision. Now that you've reached this point, you must understand that the success of your properties will now directly be the result of the management company's work. It will be worth the time to vet local companies to ensure you're working with a best-in-class business that meets your needs.

One reference for selecting a management company is the Institute of Real Estate Management (IREM) website; here, search for an individual or company with the Certified Property Manager (CPM) designation. The CPM is a designation given to management companies that have taken their courses and passed some required tests. It's not a guarantee of competency, but if you had a broken BMW, would you rather hire your cousin—the shade tree mechanic—to repair it or a mechanic with a BMW certification? Additionally, you could check out the BiggerPockets website online and go to their forums section to see if others in your area have already posted asking about management companies in your area.

Start with the list of certified managers in your area and then call around to other investors in the area or even the Better Business Bureau (BBB) to get a better understanding of how they operate. Additionally, you could request a list of some of the properties they manage and drive by them yourself to see the condition they are in. If possible, get a tenant's opinion on how the company operates and interacts with them.

Here's a quick checklist to help you frame a conversation with relevant questions in vetting a potential management company:

- ☑ Ask them about your property's market and their onboarding process. Competent management companies should know the market better than you. They should quickly be able to tell you what market rent rates would be for your properties. They should have systems and documents in place to onboard your property and tenants and make it a seamless transition.
- ☑ Discuss with them the manner and extent of the tenant screening process.
- ☑ Talk about advertising the property; who is financially responsible and what their methods are as well as their fee for tenant placement.
- ☑ Discuss maintenance and repairs to the property and how you want to navigate those waters with them.

☑ Discuss how much you will have in escrow for repairs.

☑ Discuss over what dollar amount you want to be notified, if at all, for repairs.

☑ Inquire who does their repair work.

☑ Talk about how they bid jobs and what their fees are.

☑ Ask about the response time to tenant inquiries.

☑ Ask if inspections are conducted on the property, if so, ask about the frequency of these and what they entail.

☑ Discuss how repair costs are broken down and the different service rates.

Oftentimes, management companies charge low per-unit monthly fees to draw customers. Typically, in these arrangements, the companies make more money off their service fees for repairs than they do from the management fee. You'll want to keep them honest by requiring approval in writing for repairs that may exceed a certain amount of money. This is until you feel that you can trust them not to gouge you or identify repairs that didn't necessarily need to be made. If larger jobs are required, make sure to receive several bids, and the winning bidder should supply a copy of their license and liability insurance. Require pictures of the "before and after" of the work as well.

Management companies will be responsible for collecting the rent then delivering it to you. You're never wrong for accounting for human behavior and wanting to protect yourself. There are companies with sketchy business practices. To best avoid this, ensure the rents are going into an account you and the management company are both signed onto. In the event there is a falling-out between you and the company, you'll still be able to get your money. Additionally, request a list of tenant contact information, unit number, and monthly rent roll to make sure they're not underreporting the rent and skimming from the top. Don't be afraid to call tenants to confirm they're paying if you have a hunch that something isn't right.

At the end of the day, just like training your tenants when you were first starting out, you will need to train your property management company to operate and communicate according to your preference. In lieu of your own leadership, they will carry on according to their prerogative. Remember, like old Milton Friedman said, "You can spend your own money on yourself. You can spend your own money on someone else. You can spend somebody else's money on yourself. You can spend somebody else's money on somebody else." Property management companies are receiving somebody else's money (yours) and spending it on someone else (their business or the repairmen), so they don't have the same care for each dollar spent that you would have. Their goal is to increase their bottom line, with little to no consideration for yours.

Building Your Network and Team. You can only get so far on your own, and the only way to reach new heights with your real estate business is to create a team where you leverage other people's backgrounds or specialties to dramatically reduce the amount of time it would take you to reach your goals. By now, you've probably noticed that you've managed to get started and make the initial ascent on your own. As you look to grow and scale your business, you should quickly realize that there are more effective means of getting there than having to do every function of the business yourself.

To build your team most effectively, you need to first look inward at yourself and analyze your capabilities and strategy. Reflect upon what you bring to the table: your strengths, weaknesses, desires, and dislikes. You want to be able to strengthen your weaknesses, leverage your strengths, and eliminate the distractions that keep you from attaining your vision.

The second step is to evaluate your needs. What are your limiting factors? Do you need financing? Do you need expertise in a specific niche—such as, marketing, property maintenance, property management, or administration? Come up with a list to detail altogether as many of the gaps as possible.

Once you have your list generated, identify key players for those roles. Let's say, you're limited by your ability to finance more properties. Do you need relationships with more institutions, or do you need to partner with higher net-worth individuals? Where will you find them? To help generate thought, below is a list of people from all areas within the real estate field that you may want to identify to collaborate with:

- Banks, credit unions, or private money lenders
- Contractors and specific contractors for each specialty (e.g., electricians, plumbers, carpenters, etc.)
- Property Managers
- Attorneys
- Accountants
- Marketers
- Real estate agents, wholesalers, or lead generators
- Property inspectors or appraisers
- Furniture staging companies or interior designers

Now that you've "covered down" on how you will strengthen your weaknesses and leverage your strengths, you can begin to piece together your team as you deem appropriate. Every person will be at a different stage and require a different approach, so you will need to think and come up with a plan of how to implement these relationships as mutually beneficial as possible. For example, you may be flipping properties or renovating your rentals and want to complete the project to yield the highest resale or highest rent. Maybe working with a furniture staging company would be beneficial because they could be consulted for the interior design recommendations, and—in return—your utilization of their services can help in their marketing or brand promotion. This could lay the groundwork for better pricing as well as a relationship that refers each other deals or business. Everybody is one degree away from knowing something or someone of value to you.

Just like step 8 in the Troop Leading Procedures, supervise and refine. Continuously manage and refine your relationships and efforts to create as much synergy as possible, so that one person's success will enable the success of the other. A rising tide lifts all ships.

Through assembling your team, you will be building more and more relationships which will inevitably increase your network. Always ask for a reference. You may be working with someone who is great at what they do, but never shy away from asking them who else they know that is doing what you are doing or for recommendations of people they work with in the industry that are competent. Partnerships are the way to quickly realize greater success; as you build credibility within the community and expand your network, more opportunities will avail themselves to you.

Check on Learning:

1. What are the effective property management principles?

- Leadership

- Timeliness

- Consistency

- Integrity

- Respect

- Cleanliness

- Discernment

It is important to backwards plan. Begin with the end in mind and drill down to how that will affect decisions for today, tomorrow, and in the future.

2. What are some factors to consider when selecting property management software?

- Management of property maintenance

- Integration with other solutions

- Payment collection

- Vacancy Management

- Tenant Screening

3. What are two websites you can use to vet a property management company?

- www.cpm.com

- www.biggerpockets.com

4. How will you most effectively build your team?

- Leverage your strengths

- Strengthen your weaknesses

- Evaluate your needs

Chapter 8

FIRST DEAL COMPLETED, NOW WHAT?

In this chapter, we will be going over some other benefits for service members that you can utilize to continue your growth with minimal cash out of pocket, or other niches to consider.

9 Tips for Funding Your Next Deal. Probably, the most intimidating factor in beginning your real estate investing career is money: "how much do I need?", "what do I do to get more cash?", "how much should I maintain in reserves?"

This is oftentimes the greatest limiting factor to your growth and the main reason why people say that real estate is "a slow grind to massive wealth." Yes, if you stay disciplined and consistent, twenty years down the road when you have a large portfolio that is mostly paid off, you will be swimming in Benjamins. I propose the question, why wait? If you understand what you're doing and have the capacity to do it, don't let financing be your limiting factor.

Conventional wisdom is that you should have between three to six months of your mortgage payment set aside in reserves. I'm in agreeance with this train of thought, especially when it's related to someone who is starting out. Once you reach a certain threshold (and that will be different for every person) you will gain a sense of comfort with varying levels of risk.

Amidst the COVID-19 situation, many investors were caught with their pants down and had to make rash decisions to avoid foreclosure or bankruptcy. Of course, a three-to-six-month fund would have alleviated some stress initially but would not have fully protected investors against the length of time the National Eviction Moratorium lasted. We can't plan for global pandemics—and hopefully we won't have to for the next few generations—but there is something to be said for having a safety net. If nothing else, it will give you more time to make better decisions on how to handle the situation.

As your cash flow grows and cash in the bank grows, you will be able to adjust the amount you want to have set aside or make strategic moves understanding your near- and far-term cash projections. I will now make a point with some hesitancy because I can see the dangers and pitfalls of what I'm about to say, but I also believe it will benefit those who are mature enough to hear it. If you are disciplined and responsible enough, you can forego the three-to-six-month cash reserves if you have high enough credit card limits, and those cards have low interest rates. In the spirit of growing quickly, waiting around to pile up three-to-six-months' worth of mortgage payments can take a lot of time.

If that cash can be of better service to you in the here and now by purchasing more deals or generating more cash flow through other means, understand your risk of this debt-leveraging and proceed with caution. Nowadays, just about anything can be paid for by credit card and you have thirty days to come up with the means to pay the bill. Additionally, if you have a "0% APR introductory offer" termed credit card, you can extend the bill payments out by only making minimum monthly payments until the interest rate climbs back up on the card and then try to pay it all off as quickly as possible.

Now for the 9 tips on funding your next deal:

 Tip 1: Wholesaling

One of the quickest ways to build cash in the bank without much skin in the game is through wholesaling properties. With respect to real estate investing, wholesaling is the process through which you secure a property under a contract and seek to assign that contract to a buyer. Typically, there are no realtors involved, and that's why this technique works. Ideally, the wholesaler negotiates the seller to their rock-bottom price and then markets the deal to his or her (the wholesaler's) network with an assignment fee built in, such that the end buyer still receives a good deal. This can be done for flips, rentals, or permanent residences. An example of wholesaling a distressed property to a flipper would look like the following:

You find a motivated seller willing to work directly with you for the purchase of their home. You agree to a forty-five-day close in your contract which includes a clause allowing assignment of the contract. You are able to lock the property down for $85,000. After walking through the property and conducting some good due diligence, you estimate that the property would be worth $175,000 after about $40,000 in repairs.

You identify a buyer for $95,000 and find yourself a win-win solution. You make $10,000 without lifting a single hammer, and the flipper is still purchasing the property with enough margin to make a worthwhile return on his or her investment. If this model sounds interesting to you, I highly advise learning about the legalities in your specific state when it comes to structuring these transactions.

Tip 2: Conventional Financing

There are many means to quickly getting cash together to fund your next deal. For conventional methods, banks and credit unions. A thing to note about using banks is that you will gain much more traction using local banks than the national chains. National chain banks are strictly regulated and have guidelines that they are oftentimes unable to waver from in order to work with your situation. Local banks aren't bound by all the same standards and are therefore abler to make deals work for you. Likewise, credit unions charge much lower fees and have a vested interest in the community they're a part of. Typically, they even have a specific radius they prefer to lend in. You'll come to see that they have more and more flexible loan products to meet your needs than traditional banks. Ask to speak with lenders at these local banks and credit unions to learn what loan products they have available. Introduce yourself and begin to build relationships with them by informing them of your background, what you're currently doing, and where you're headed.

Tip 3: Hard Money Lenders

"Loan shark" is a term used to describe persons or companies that loan at extremely high interest rates, have strict terms of collection upon default, and operate outside of local lending authority. Payday loans or title loans fit this description. You want to stay away from these organizations. Hard money lenders are not as "sharky" as what was previously described, but they do charge higher percentages and have stricter collection terms than banks do. They can get away with this structure because, for a wide variety of reasons, people that are unable to qualify for traditional bank loans may be eligible for hard money loans.

Hard money loans are more commonly used for flip properties than rental properties, but each situation will be different. They can also be used as bridge-financing between buying a property and securing a longer-term loan from another source. Hard money lenders can also be a good litmus test as to whether you're purchasing a good deal. They will be frank with you, and either the discussion or the loan terms will inform you of the risk they perceive. They're in the business to make money after all, so they may give you the financing for your endeavor or advice against going forth with your deal. If traditional banks turn you down, hard money lenders turn you down, and even other investors advise against the deal—you probably have a bad deal. There's plenty of bad deals out there, so don't be surprised if this happens. Fortunately, there are tons of good deals out there as well, so keep pushing towards finding that next best deal.

 Tip 4: Private Money Lenders

If you're fortunate enough to have people in your life with cash lying around—such as, family members, friends, colleagues, or business professionals, borrowing from them is considered private lending. There's typically nowhere near as much of a process to borrowing from these folks as there is for borrowing from hard money lenders or banks. It's entirely upon you to make the arrangements of the deal, and I strongly recommend having an attorney review it because even the best of intentions can turn into a burnt relationship, and you want to avoid that at all costs.

Tip 5: Crowdfunding and Peer-to-Peer Lending

I don't have personal experience with either of these, but I'm including them as options because I've known other people to use them successfully. Crowdfunding is a platform that you can contribute to for a Return on Investment (ROI) on your own dollars that you have contributed, or you can set one up for people to contribute to your campaign. Note that this is unlikely a good option for someone with minimal or no track record. You would probably be skeptical about lending your hard-earned money to someone with only one or two deals under their belt, right? Now, peer-to-peer lending matches you with an investor who then loans you the funds for your project, and you pay back with interest. There's a lot of variety in the terms and options for using peer-to-peer lending, so your experiences and results may vary. However, similar to hard money lending and crowdfunding, your loan terms will be better based on how good your deal is and how much credibility you have with previous deals.

Tip 6: Cash-Out Refinancing

These types of products typically are only an option once you have a significant amount of equity in a property whether from loan paydown or market appreciation. The Cash-Out Refinance terms vary based on your credit and the market, but often you can count on 75–85% range for Loan-to-Value (LTV) ratio, though I've seen banks go as high as 125% in the past. So, what happens is, you will get a new mortgage for a larger amount than the existing mortgage, and you will get the difference between the new and existing in cash. For example, you owe $120,000 on your property and it appraises for $200,000. At 80% LTV you should have access to:

- ($200,000) x (80%) = $160,000 new mortgage amount
- ($160,000) – ($120,000) = $40,000 cash

Your new mortgage would be $160,000, and you would have $40,000 in cash.

The first cash-out refinance I did was from three single-family homes I had under one commercial mortgage. I purchased the properties with 30% equity in them the day I signed the documents, but the market had appreciated by the time I was ready to refinance, so I had access to more equity. After that, I purchased three more single-family homes and refinanced into a blanket commercial loan for all six homes that had a lower interest rate and amortization schedule. The bank I was working with was only able to offer 75% LTV, but even still, the other win was the fact that I only had to come up with $11,000 out of my pocket to purchase the last three homes, which were also about 20% under market value!

 Tip 7: Home Equity Line of Credit (HELOC).

A HELOC allows you to borrow money from the bank using the equity in your home as collateral. It differs from the cash-out refinance in the fact that you are not remortgaging; you are essentially getting a separate loan that is based on your home's equity. For example, if you had $50,000 available to you in a HELOC, you could use that money to purchase another property. Your payments will be based on whatever the interest rate is, amount of the loan, and length of the loan. The payments will discontinue whenever you pay off the balance in full. One thing to note is that you only pay interest on what you borrow, so if you have $50,000 available but only take out $20,000, you only pay interest on the $20,000. Interest rates on HELOC are typically lower than other home loans because the lender's risk is lower as they have a track record of your timely mortgage payments and already own the note for your house.

 Tip 8: Partnership

Partnerships are not a one-size-fits-all deal, many different variations are possible and can accommodate each person's situation. The most important aspect is finding someone who is trustworthy and complimentary to your skill sets. Whether that be financing, strategy, finding the deals, managing the project or operations—they should be bringing to the table whatever you're lacking or need assistance with.

The classic example is a fifty-fifty split for cash investor and the flipper. The cash partner injects all the capital required, the other partner does all the work himself or manages the project, and they split their profits or roll into more deals maintaining a fair equity share. Partnerships can either lead to burnt bridges and damaged relationships or to even greater success; be wise in choosing whom you deal with, always protect yourself with an attorney, and practice open communication prior to engaging in anything. Remember, 10% of a deal is better than 100% of no deal.

Tip 9: Syndication

Syndication is like a partnership, but it typically involves several partners and a structure that includes general and limited partners. The syndicator raises money from investors, puts the deal together, collects a finder's fee or asset management fee, and runs the operation truly like a business. He can choose to invest his own money or acquire equity stake in the property by achieving specific performance metrics. These types of arrangements are generally best served for large apartment deals, but I have seen them done on single-family homes. As you gain in sophistication, the syndication method will likely become a weapon in your arsenal. However, keep in mind, the more people included in a deal, the more phone calls you will be receiving when investors are stressed and the more headaches to deal with, so be sure to identify if the juice is worth the squeeze on the deal in consideration.

Alternative Service-Related Home-Buying Solutions

Most of this book has focused on what you can do starting with your traditional VA Loan. This next section will cover similar loan products from Navy

Federal Credit Union, the SBA, and a VA Construction Loan.

Navy Federal Credit Union Loans. This product functions similarly to the VA Loan in the fact that it can be 100% financed, which means little to no money down and no Private Mortgage Insurance (PMI) is required. In addition, the seller can contribute up to 6% of the value of the home towards closing costs. I have noticed that the interest rates for this product are usually about 1–1.5% higher than VA Loan guaranteed rates. Be sure to speak with a lender and confirm what interest rate you will be receiving, their funding fee percentage, and what your closing costs will be—and, of course, do your due diligence. Navy Federal lists the following as eligible for membership: Active-Duty members, Delayed Entry Program, DoD Officer Candidates/ROTC, DoD Reservists, veterans, retirees, and annuitants. Additionally, DoD civilian employees, US Government employees assigned to DoD installations, DoD contractors assigned to US Government installations, and DoD civilian retirees and annuitants.

The main difference between this Navy Federal product and the VA Loan is that the VA permits the purchase of up to a 4-unit home. The Navy Federal product is specifically for single-family homes. However, the guidelines are much more flexible as to the condition and criteria of the property. If it is structurally sound and you intend to live in it, this loan will enable you to get into a home. So, you could easily use this loan to eventually flip a property.

Military Choice Loan. Additionally, there is the Military Choice Loan, another Navy Federal product, that is a good option for those that have already exhausted their VA Loan benefit by having multiple VA Loans out concurrently or another circumstance that may preclude you from use of another VA Loan. The interest rates are slightly better with this product compared with the Navy Federal Home Buyers Choice Loan. However, many of the loan features remain the same.

The strategy behind utilizing the VA Loan and Navy Federal Loan:

If you have the presence of mind to think in terms of several moves ahead, you should note that if you intend to incorporate a Navy Federal Loan product in addition to your VA Loan, you need to be smart about how you set it up. The VA Loan has stricter requirements and regulations, so I would advise getting your first home using the VA Loan. Technically, you could purchase a 4-unit property with your VA Loan and then a single-family with your Navy Federal Loan thus giving you five units for practically no money down. If you purchase a home with the Navy Federal product first, you may find it harder to secure a VA Loan in the same zip code because the VA Loan intent is to have you use the home as a primary residence. Consequently, you will have a less favorable Debt-to-Income (DTI) ratio from already having a home through Navy Federal. Navy Federal isn't as strict in their requirements and permits you to have a home in the same locale. For this reason, I would suggest the following:

Buy a multiunit property with a VA Loan and live in it for a year. During that time, be on the hunt for your next deal and utilize the Navy Federal (no money down) loan for your next property. Hopefully, you purchased a good deal with some equity already in it and realized some loan paydown from collecting rent. Now you can refinance out of your VA Loan into a conventional product, which then frees up your entire VA eligibility again. You could do it this way, or if you get reassigned elsewhere, use your remaining VA eligibility to purchase another home in another area with a second VA Loan.

If executed in the manner described, you could potentially have up to nine units within a couple years at little to no money down. You can continuously repeat this process. Maybe you've been accumulating more cash from a work promotion, saving, side-hustling, or generating rental cash flow to start accelerating your acquisition time frames. The VA funding fee increases after your initial purchase unless you have a disability rating—so keep that in mind. However, you can wrap that fee into your loan.

VA Small Business Administration (SBA) Loan: Mixed Commercial Use. Another great benefit to service members is the VA SBA Loan. This loan is not made by the VA, but it is partially guaranteed by the Small Business Administration (SBA). The loan will originate at a bank or credit union, but the SBA will guarantee 50% of the loan, leaving the bank to finance 40%, and you—the business owner—will only have to finance 10%.

Who is eligible for the VA SBA Loan? Honorably discharged veterans, service-disabled veterans, active-duty service members eligible for the Transition Assistance Program (TAP), reservists, and spouses of the above. The business must be at least 51% owned by a qualified veteran and used for profit— and it cannot be a pyramid scheme, gambling business, or lending business.

The strategy behind utilizing the SBA Loan for rental properties:

If you have made a business out of a side hustle or in fact do have a business, 51% of the property square footage must be intended for business use, basements are included in this number. A perfect application would be a mixed-commercial-use property. A mixed-commercial-use typically has a storefront and a couple apartment units attached to the building. You don't need to have a history of owning a business; this loan can be utilized to purchase a property for a business you are creating—even a property management company.

The lender's requirements for business plans will vary, but they can be very simple and very straightforward: inquiries on what the nature of the business is, what you estimate expenses to be, how you expect to earn revenue, and if you can provide a very rough estimate of a profit schedule. The sky is the limit for your creativity as to what you could use that space for to generate income. The nice thing is that the lender will incorporate the attached rental unit income to help you qualify for the loan.

VA Construction Loan. Construction loans are riskier by nature and each VA lender will have varying levels of determinations of risks and availability to offer these types of loans. You may find that more lenders are inclined to let you purchase the land and utilize a conventional construction loan until project completion, then refinance that loan into a permanent VA Loan. You can't use the VA Loan to purchase unimproved land. Depending on the bank, you may be able to use the VA Loan to purchase land that already has electric, sewer, and water running on it.

This loan product is very specific but at the same time is a gray area for many lenders. Just because one bank tells you "No," don't become defeated and give up. Through calling several places, you may be able to negotiate a way to meet your intent. If you choose the route of traditional financing in hopes of converting to a VA Loan, know that the VA will require that the home be constructed by a builder with a valid VA Builder ID. The home is still subject to VA appraisal once completed; however, you can coordinate with the appraiser to discuss your home's plans and specifications before breaking ground to get a ballpark estimate of where it should appraise at. Hopefully, there will be less or no surprises at final inspection to reach the same number.

There is an additional grant available if you have a disability, called the Specially Adapted Housing (SAH) grant. This grant can work in conjunction with your VA Loan to help cover the costs to modify a home to make it more accessible and provide barrier-free living.

After exhausting VA Benefits. Once you've diligently exhausted all available service-related benefits to build your empire, you'll find that you've established a track record, a credibility, and a network in the industry—and even potentially partners or future investors. From this point, it is up to you to research and discover the most effective means to continue to grow and scale your business. You may end up using commercial lending, private money lending, partnerships, syndications, or a combination of all the above. You are your own limiting factor, so don't get in your own way!

Check on Learning:

1. How much is a good buffer to maintain in cash reserves for rental properties?

- 3-6 months mortgage payments

2. What are some sources you can use to fund your next deal?

- Conventional lenders such as banks and credit unions

- Hard money lenders

- Private money lenders

- Crowdfunding

- Cash-Out Refinancing

- HELOC

- Partnerships

- Syndications

3. What institution offers another service related no money down loan?

- Navy Federal Credit Union

Chapter 9

EMPIRE BUILDING

Finding your financial freedom number. My goal in writing this book is to provide the information to enable you to achieve financial security and financial freedom. It is a mindset shift to realize there is a significant cap on your potential and quality of life from trading your hours for dollars. Once you can allow money to work for you and earn you more money that is not dependent on how much time you exchange to yield those dollars, you will have options. Options are energizing.

They reduce and relieve stress, allow you to focus your thoughts and energy on higher output activities and goals, and fundamentally change the way you look at the world. Changing your thought patterns from "I can't" to "how can I?" can have an inexplicable effect on the amount of success and freedom you will attain. The path of real estate investing should lead you to a point where your passive income through rental properties exceeds your living expenses. Once attained, your mental and physical bandwidth is freed up to pursue a lifestyle designed by you, not defined to you.

First things first, if you can't measure it, you can't manage it. You need to gain an attention to detail regarding your finances that will illuminate poor spending habits, identify areas for improvement, and inform where your spending aligns with your values. Take a good, hard look at your spending history over the past few months and have a reality check with yourself. Ask yourself if this spending behavior is detracting from or aligning you with the goals you have for your financial future.

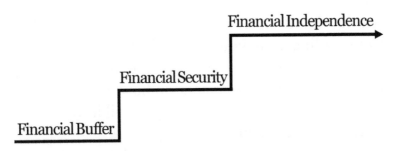

Leveling up to financial independence:

Financial Buffer. Your first step on this path is creating a financial buffer. Through the lens of real estate, a buffer would mean having enough cash flow coming in monthly to sustain you through a layoff or a transition in between jobs. You may have to adapt your lifestyle and tighten your budget, but you will have the breathing room to make better decisions and have the time to wait for the right job instead of the right now job. This can eliminate so much stress in the unfortunate event something like that were to occur. You can picture this as a number equal to what your monthly rent or mortgage payment is. You can later recover from late utility payments and use credit cards to stay afloat for food and survival needs but getting too far behind on mortgage payments could be a very stressful and dangerously compromising position.

Financial Security. Once you've built a cash flow that can carry you through rocky times, the next goal is to increase that cash flow to cover your fixed living expenses—financial security. If your rental portfolio was enough to let you save every dollar you earn from your day job, how freeing would that feel? How much sooner would you be able to achieve the financial goals you have in place or even take that vacation you've been longing for? Even if you were to stop at this point, you would be miles ahead of your peers in terms of quality of life. Did you know that, according to a survey conducted by CareerBuilder, seventy-eight percent of all employees in the United States live paycheck to paycheck? Only thirty-seven percent of adults have any funds accumulated for an emergency or unexpected expense and would have to dip into their savings, and sixty-nine percent of people surveyed had $1,000 or less in their savings account.

To calculate how much you need for financial security, first identify what you spend monthly on rent or mortgage, utilities, phone, food, and insurance. You can take one month's example as a rough estimate or do a detailed analysis of what your average monthly expense is. Take that monthly number and multiply it by twelve for your annual cost. You may be surprised to see how expensive or inexpensive it is to live your current lifestyle, and you can potentially make some course-correcting changes to align yourself more with your goals.

Financial Independence. Reaching this level equates to being able to cover all your fixed monthly expenses and discretionary spending—such as, clothing, entertainment, and lifestyle. The premise of this level is that you wouldn't need to work if you didn't want to. This can be as wide of a spectrum as you permit it to be. If you live a lifestyle well beneath your means and have a conservative mindset, you could reach this position quicker than if you tend to spend money like it grows on trees.

For this number, look over everything you've spent money on over the past twelve months and discard the larger one-time purchases or holiday spending, you're looking for patterns. Find what each month's amount is and then average them together. Once averaged, pad that number by 15%. An example may be that you find you spend on average $3,000 a month to live your lifestyle. Pad it by 15%, so add $450. You want to pad it to protect yourself in the event you have costly repairs on a rental one month or need to spend more for your personal life. You're now looking to cash flow $3,450 a month.

How will you get there? Let's look at how many rental properties could fulfill that requirement. Your deals will determine how quickly or slowly this can be achieved, so just use this as a general reference. If you know you're averaging $350 per month of net cash flow per unit from your properties, it will take ten units to achieve your financial independence goal.

That number would change if you're earning $600 per unit per month, then it would only take six units. That could be as doable as getting one 4-unit property with the VA Loan, a single-family home with the Navy Federal Loan, and renting out a bedroom in your personal residence! That sounds achievable within three years, right?

Investing Models. *"Riches are made in the niches."* I believe that knowledge provides the foundation for creativity and from there, wealth. If you are informed about a subject matter, you're able to look at it in a three-dimensional way and maybe uncover a new or unmet need that you can meet or improve upon. If you are doing what everyone else is doing, you'll receive what everyone else is receiving. However, if you find a niche in the market that you have an advantage in, go all in and squeeze every ounce of profit out of it.

Until now, this book has only covered traditional real estate investing through single- or multifamily home flips or rentals. That is simply scratching the surface of possibilities in this industry. This section will briefly describe ten investing models that have proven to be effective, simply as material for your own idea generation.

Model 1: Rental arbitrage. The premise of this investing strategy is to rent a property from a landlord and sublet it to another party. For example, with the rise of Airbnb, you may find that you are able to rent a unit for $1,200 a month in an area that attracts varying levels of tourism or Airbnb demand. Furnishing the unit at your own expense, you find that you can realize an Airbnb revenue of $1,700 a month.

The spread is yours to keep. Of course, be sure to subtract your operating expenses such as utilities, Wi-Fi, cleaning services, etc. You may find that you are able to scale this and realize the same cash flow as purchasing a rental home in your own name, but for a fraction of the initial investment. Your startup cost is whatever the security deposit is plus the costs to furnish. It would be very realistic to think you could get into a property for less than $5,000 and immediately begin earning cash flow. It's also a win for the owner of the property because you or the service you hire will be giving the property a good cleaning between guests and ensuring everything is working properly, as you will be unable to sustain Airbnb'ng if it is being neglected.

Model 2: Temporary Duty Travel (TDY) Rentals. Are you aware of a location that your branch of service frequently sends service members to for longer TDY durations? If you can conduct your own market research and analysis to deem the effectiveness of purchasing a rental in that location and find a good deal, it could prove to be very profitable. You will operate it similarly to an Airbnb, incentivizing the service member to stay at your location as opposed to a hotel. You'll research what the per diem rate is or can base your cash flow projections on receiving an amount below the per diem rate to compete with the Defense Travel System (DTS) suggested lodging options.

Model 3: College towns. College towns oftentimes yield some of the highest rent rates of the different niches because you have limited supply, high demand, and can charge by the bedroom. While the cash flow projections look appealing, bear in mind that you will likely incur yearly turnover expenses due to off-campus regulations, friend groups dissolving, or students quitting school. Depending on how "rowdy" the tenants were, you may find damages costlier than the security deposit protects you from. There are many ways to run campus properties effectively. I recommend speaking with other landlords in the area and some property management companies to understand the timing of their marketing, language to incorporate in the leases, and lessons learned over the years.

Model 4: Rent by the room. You will have to consult your township codes and guidelines, but significant earnings can be realized by renting a larger home by the room. This type of scenario is like renting to college students or a large employer that has interim employee stays. It may be that in your area, your 5-bedroom property would typically rent for $1,500 a month. With the ability to rent by the room, you find that you can charge $450 a month per room, realizing a rent of $2,250 a month. You most likely will have to pay utilities unless you have a home layout that is conducive to individual metering, and it would be advisable to pay for a cleaning service to keep tenant tensions low. There are many ways to go about utilizing this strategy but know that it will be management-intensive, as there is typically a much higher turnover rate. The home will most likely be filled with strangers, so there's no way to foresee the potential reasons for the phone calls you will or may receive.

Model 5: Long-term single-family homes. This will be the most stable form of income you'll likely find when it comes to rental properties. Finding a good, hardworking family that treats your property with respect and may live there for five, ten, or twenty years and never miss a payment is the ideal setup. You want to be sure to establish a good relationship with these tenants. The amount of money you'll save over the years from not having to incur in expenses related to turnover, repairs, or marketing will add up. Oftentimes, if a family is in a home long enough, they take ownership and will fix things on their own, and you'll notice you'll have less phone calls from them, less headaches, and simply mailbox money. The only downside with this strategy is factoring in your pricing. You don't want to aggressively increase rents because you may lose out on good tenants and find yourself with new tenants that give ten times the headache—for such a slight rent bump, it's not worth it.

Model 6: Land. Depending on which part of the country you are considering, land can be a profitable, cash-flowing asset. Many times, people in major metropolitan areas have hobbies like—for example, dirt biking, hunting, fishing, shooting, or camping and want to have their own land to do those hobbies on. Land is typically not given as favorable financing terms as a home is, so you may find purchasing in cash or lease options will get you more opportunities. Similarly, your target tenant demographic probably doesn't have the cash to purchase the property outright either. Utilizing a lease with option to buy is one of the most common ways to structure land deals. You will have them give you a down payment and negotiate a monthly amortization schedule that either pays off the property or has a balloon payment after a certain amount of time that completes the transaction. If they default, you get to keep it and repeat the process. Otherwise, it is maintenance-free mailbox money.

Model 7: Commercial Real Estate (CRE). Some examples of commercial real estate include retail stores, offices, hotels, or industrial applications (e.g., manufacturing sites, warehouses, car washes, storage facilities, schools, and apartments). Commercial loans also differ from residential loans. Typically, commercial loans are for shorter lengths of time and have adjustable rates, which are typically higher than residential rates. You may have a 20-year payment amortization schedule, but your interest rate is only guaranteed for the first five years, then you'll have to refinance out. The terms can be much more flexible than with residential loans. For example, there are interest-only loans for certain amounts of time that lead to a balloon payment. Lending for commercial properties doesn't necessarily have to be from a bank either. This is the space for joint ventures, private capital, and opportunity-zone incentives. The benefits of investing into commercial real estate as opposed to residential real estate include factors such as:

- Higher income from higher rent premiums, lower vacancy, and long-term leases. Typically, tenants pay for maintenance, tax, utilities, and insurance.

- Less competition, this space is more sophisticated and is not flooded with inexperienced investors like the residential market is.
- Opportunity for network or business expansion. If you are renting a warehouse to a growing company, you may find opportunity to partner or invest in their business and yield even more returns in addition to the rent you receive.
- Low likelihood of 24/7 phone calls from tenants. Due to the nature of the businesses or the fact that most of them manage their own maintenance, there is relatively little chance that you will receive middle-of-the-night calls about toilets leaking.
- Opportunity-zone tax incentives. Certain parts of the city will give advantageous tax treatment to businesses that come to the area, funds that invest in housing or improving the housing, and much more.

Model 8: Garages. In growing downtown or sometimes even suburban areas, space is in high demand. People need garages for a host of reasons, but you may find opportunity in renting a garage separately from a property you own, or even finding a garage for sale by itself and realizing rental income from that. You always have the option to build an addition to the garage and possibly convert it into a studio apartment or additional space to charge higher rent.

Model 9: Off-street parking. Like the need for garages, people pay premium for convenience. If you own land or parking rights in a specific area, you may find you're able to make some money leasing it to someone else. Even if you live in an apartment complex and have two spots assigned to you when you only use one—you can still make a profit.

Model 10: Apartments and mobile home parks. These asset classes deserve their own book because of how in-depth the information can get. In short, the more units on one property, the better. If you have a 20-unit apartment building and raise rent by fifty dollars per unit, you just increased your income by $1,000 a month while also increasing the value of the apartment. Values are derived from the gross rents. If you purchased a property that was a little run-down or under-rented and fixed it up bringing rents to market rate, you may find that you built for yourself several hundred-thousand dollars of equity.

Check on Learning:

1. How do you find your financial freedom number?
Identify annual expenses

- Multiply by 15%

- Calculate how many rental properties you would need based on their average cash flow to exceed that number.

2. What are some additional real estate investing models?

- Rental arbitrage

- TDY rentals

- College towns

- Rent by the room

- Long-term single-family homes

- Land

- Commercial real estate

- Garages

- Off-street parking

- Apartments and mobile home parks

Chapter 10

A FINAL WORD

I read seventy-five books on my first deployment to Afghanistan, listened to hundreds of hours of podcasts and YouTube videos, and made countless phone calls with experts in their disciplines. All this taught me 1,000 times more than anything I learned from four years in college to get a degree in Finance. One of my biggest takeaways from all my personal growth and self-education is that you need to get your mind right before your success can take flight. There is nothing too difficult in life; most everything can be broken down to simple concepts or steps. Real estate investing may seem intimidating at first, but your fear is of the unknown.

Once you educate yourself, take action, and begin the process, you make known the unknown and will quickly realize your mind is your only limiting factor. Success has no rules or traditions you must adhere to.

There is nothing stopping you from reading this book and then purchasing a multi-million-dollar warehouse or large apartment because you understood the concepts, surrounded yourself with the right people, and executed a plan. You could simply be one move or one relationship away from great financial gain. How you do one thing is how you do everything. That mantra applies to success as well because if you have achieved a new mindset and realized success in one area of your life, the principles and new behavior will carry over and grow the other aspects of your life. It all begins with creating a vision for yourself then boiling that vision down into interim goals and subtasks from which you can generate daily tasks to create momentum.

Identify what you need to learn, how to learn it, and the one thing necessary to do each day that will create a domino effect for the attainment of your goal. I could go on and fill another book with motivation and inspiration themed messaging, but I recommend you learn from others as well to add more tools to your toolbox. Start your reading through this list with the books and resources about mindset first.

Mindset

- *Rich Dad, Poor Dad* – Robert Kiyosaki and Sharon Lechter
- *The Miracle Morning* – Hal Elrod
- *Ultralearning: Master Hard Skills, Outsmart the Competition, and Accelerate Your Career* – Scott H. Young
- *Mentored by a Millionaire: Master Strategies of Super Achievers* – Steven K. Scott
- *The Richest Man Who Ever Lived: King Solomon's Secrets to Success, Wealth, and Happiness* – Steven K. Scott
- *Think and Grow Rich* – Napoleon Hill
- *The 4-hour workweek: Escape the 9-5, Live Anywhere and Join the New Rich* – Timothy Ferris
- *How to Win Friends and Influence People* – Dale Carnegie
- *The 10x Rule: The Only Difference Between Success and Failure* – Grant Cardone
- *The 7 Habits of Highly Effective People* – Stephen R. Covey
- *Your Next 5 Moves: Master the Art of Business Strategy* – Patrick Bet-David

Tax

- *IRS Tax Code.*
- *The Book on Tax Strategies for the Savvy Real Estate Investor: Powerful techniques anyone can use to deduct more, invest smarter, and pay far less*

to the IRS. – Amanda Hann and Matthew MacFarland
- *Tax-Free Wealth: How to Build Massive Wealth by Permanently Lowering Your Taxes* – Tom Wheelwright, CPA
- *Real Estate Loopholes: Secrets of Successful Real Estate Investing* – Dianne Kennedy and Garrett Sutton

Negotiation

- *Trump: The Art of the Deal* – Donald Trump and Tony Schwartz
- *Never Split the Difference: Negotiating as if Your Life Depended on It* –Christopher Voss and Tahl Raz
- *Getting More: How You Can Negotiate to Succeed in Work and Life* – Stuart Diamond
- *The Sweet Art of Negotiation* – Paul Wineman
- *The Challenger Sale: Taking Control of the Customer Conversation* – Matthew Dixon

Real Estate Investing

- *Investing in Duplexes, Triplexes, and Quads: The Fastest and Safest Way to Real Estate Wealth* – Larry B. Loftis
- *The Book on Flipping Houses: How to Buy, Rehab, and Resell Residential Properties* – J. Scott
- *The Unofficial Guide to Real Estate Investing* – Spencer Strauss and Martin Stone

- *Best Ever Apartment Syndication Book: A Four-Part System for Raising Money and Buying Apartments* – Joe Fairless and Theo Hicks
- *The Millionaire Real Estate Investor* – Gary Keller, Dave Jenks, and Jay Papasan
- *What Every Real Estate Investor Needs to Know About Cash Flow... And 36 Other Key Financial Measures* – Frank Gallinelli
- *Building Wealth One House at a Time* – John W. Schaub
- *Buy, Rent, Rehab, Refinance, Repeat: The BRRRR Rental Property Investment Strategy Made Simple* – David Greene
- *The Book on Investing in Real Estate with No or Low Money Down: Real Life Strategies for Investing in Real Estate Using Other People's Money* – Brandon Turner
- *Build a Rental Property Empire: The No-Nonsense Book on Finding Deals, Financing the Right Way, and Managing Wisely* – Mark Ferguson

ABOUT THE AUTHOR

Michael Balboa is a Green Beret, author, entrepreneur, and active real estate investor. Though he has a Finance degree from Ohio University and experience on Wall Street, he has learned more about building personal wealth from reading hundreds of books, receiving mentorship, and taking timely, decisive action on that information. Through relationships, partnerships, and marksmanship, Michael is passionate about empowering others with the lessons he's learned and enriching the lives of other veterans.

**Scan to leave a review for
Break Rank, Make Bank**

Find more helpful
content and resources at
The Cash Flow Commando Webpage

CONNECT WITH THE CASH FLOW COMMANDO

and begin your journey to Making Bank today!

Facebook
/cashflowcommander

Instagram
@thecashflowcommando

Twitter
@cashflowcmdr

Pinterest
/CashFlowCommander

thecashflowcommando.com

Connect with Blacksmith Publishing

Books by Blacksmith Publishing

Small Unit Tactics Handbook

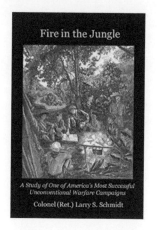

Fire in the Jungle

Land Navigation From Start to Finish

Tactical Leadership

Books by Blacksmith Publishing

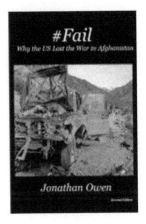

 # Fail

Confederate Black Ops

Active Shooter Awareness and Response

Marriage is a Four-Letter Word

Books by Blacksmith Publishing

God's Man

Iron Sharpening Iron

Unto the Thousandth Generation

Triple Canopy

Books by Blacksmith Publishing

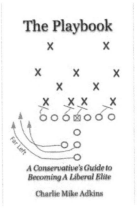

Break Rank Make Bank

The Playbook

www.blacksmithpublishingcom

Lightning Source UK Ltd.
Milton Keynes UK
UKHW040652040122
396592UK00003B/331